TELLING GOD'S STORY

YEAR TWO: THE KINGDOM OF HEAVEN

INSTRUCTOR TEXT AND TEACHING GUIDE

Telling God's Story

Year Two: The Kingdom of Heaven

Instructor Text and Teaching Guide

Peter Enns

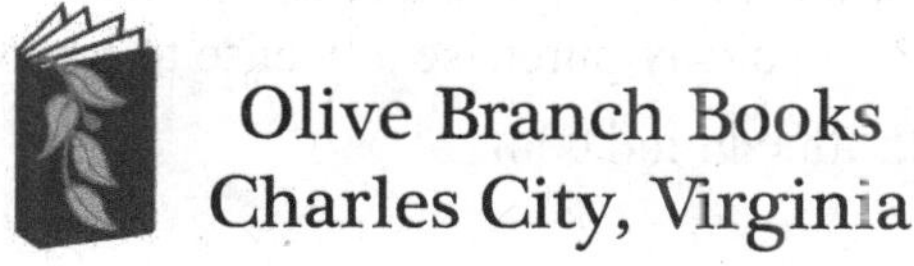

Olive Branch Books
Charles City, Virginia

This book is to be used in conjunction with *Telling God's Story: Year Two Student Guide and Activity Pages* (ISBN 978-1-933339-51-1), available at www.olivebranchbooks.net or wherever books are sold.

Cover design by Mike Fretto and Mollie Bauer.

Publisher's Cataloging-In-Publication Data
(Prepared by The Donohue Group, Inc.)

Enns, Peter, 1961-
    Telling God's story. Year Two, The kingdom of heaven : instructor text and teaching guide / Peter Enns.

        p. ; cm.

    Interest grade level: 2.
    "This book is to be used in conjunction with Telling God's story: year two student guide and activity pages."
    ISBN: 978-1-933339-50-4

    1. Jesus Christ--Biography--Study and teaching (Primary) 2. Jesus Christ--Teachings--Study and teaching (Primary) 3. Jesus Christ--Miracles--Study and teaching (Primary) I. Title.

BT207 .E56 2012 Year2 TchrMan
232

2 3 4 5 6 7 8 9 10   MER   30 29 28 27 26 25 24 23 22
WTM100422

Table of Contents

                                                      Contents

Unit 8: The End of Jesus' Life

Supplemental Lessons: The Rest of the Story

Introduction

The Bible is primarily a God-centered story. It is not designed to be a "Book of Virtues" but a book that tells us who God is and what he has done. The Bible, in other words, is a story that begins with the dysfunction of the early chapters of Genesis, moves to God's dealings with a particular group of people—his chosen people, the Israelites—and then culminates in what God did through Jesus of Nazareth.

Who Jesus is and what he did is central to the Christian faith. That is why this curriculum begins with teaching children about Jesus. Of course, much of who Jesus is and what he did is rooted in the Old Testament, and we will certainly get to that—but in due time. It is good to remember that the first followers of Jesus were likely far less familiar with the Old Testament than we might think. There were no printed books back then. Peter and the others, when they were called by Jesus to follow him, did not have their Bibles open and may not even have been all that familiar with the Scripture's content.

When Jesus came on the scene he did not say, "OK, before I begin talking, please open up your Bibles and let me show you how all of this fits together." Rather, he came on the scene and just started being Jesus. And the point was made well enough.

So we will follow this pattern: beginning this curriculum by acquainting children with Jesus first and then letting the rest of the Bible fall into place. We are intentionally avoiding the "Bible story" approach, which starts with creation, Adam and Eve, the flood, etc., as the basis of moral lessons. We are beginning at the culmination of the story, to see how all of this ends up—acquainting children with the most central truths of the Scripture before we go back to fill in the many interesting details.

A much fuller explanation of the methods behind this program is found in the core text for this series, *Telling God's Story: A Parents' Guide to Teaching the Bible.*

Organization

The lessons for Years One through Four are centered on understanding Jesus: who he was, what he did, and what he taught. The lessons organize the Gospel story into nine categories:

Stories Jesus Told
Miracles Jesus Did
Teachings of Jesus
Sermon on the Mount
Jesus' Early Life
Jesus' Disciples
Opposition to Jesus
End of Jesus' Life
The Rest of the Story

Aim to complete one lesson per week. You may wish to read the scripted lesson to the child on the first day as he or she colors the picture, and then to complete projects on the second and third days. Alternately, you may read the scripted lesson on the first day, complete the coloring picture on the second, and complete a chosen project on the third. In a group setting that meets once a week, plan to read the scripted lesson as the students color and then to conclude the day's study with one of the projects especially designed for group use.

Each of these categories has four or five lessons, which means that you will spend four or five weeks on each category. The order is not unalterable, but neither is it random. We start with the stories Jesus told (parables) because this is one way that Jesus introduced himself to the people of his day. He also introduced himself through miracles and his various teachings, which are second and third on the list. These are the ways the people of Jesus' world got to know him, and it is a good way to introduce Jesus to your children, too.

The fourth category, the "Sermon on the Mount," is really a subset of the previous category ("Teachings of Jesus"). The Sermon on the Mount is so rich and well known, however, that it deserves a separate treatment. So, the first four categories have one thing in common: they all pertain to what Jesus did and said to the people of his day. These were the ways people got to know him.

The next five categories are more biographical. Here the lessons will focus more on Jesus' life, beginning with his birth, then moving to his relationship with his disciples, the opposition he faced toward the end of his earthly ministry, and culminating in his death and resurrection. These categories are also important for children to get to know Jesus. Young students are often not taught the Gospel accounts of Jesus' life in a way that shows just how interesting and challenging the Biblical message is. These last four categories will question some preconceptions, and therefore deepen our understanding of who Jesus is.

Even though the order of the lessons is very intentional, parents should feel free to alter the order to suit their own purposes. For example, you might decide to work through "Jesus' Early Life" during the Christmas season and "End of Jesus' Life" during Easter. The only strong suggestion we make is that each category be completed before moving onto another so that the lessons have a stronger sense of continuity ("Next we are going to look at the miracles for Jesus for five weeks").

The purpose of this curriculum is to get to know Jesus better. In fact, it is very likely that as parents or teachers, you may find yourself re-introduced to Jesus in a fresh way. This is why each lesson opens with a short reading that explains the passage to the instructor; this will help you in helping your children process the content of the lessons.

Toward that end, you should spend a few moments reading the parent section ("What the Parent Should Know") the night before the lesson so you can ponder a bit, or if you prefer, read it right before the lesson so it is fresh in your mind—whatever works for you. The important thing is that you spend some time becoming familiar with the information so you can be of more help to your children. The purpose of these parent sections is to orient you to the biblical passage for that day. The parent sections are more detailed and complex than the scripted lessons; this will give you a broader handle on the issues surrounding each passage. It will also give you a greater vantage point from which to look at the lesson itself, and, perhaps, to address questions that might come up.

All Scriptural excerpts are drawn from the New International Version except where otherwise noted.

Scope

Jesus is the primary subject of this curriculum for the first four years. We want to encourage parents and teachers not to feel as if the child's biblical education is being truncated by focusing on Jesus. Rather, *Telling*

God's Story allows young students to get to know the central figure of the Christian faith in a way that conventional curricula do not do.

But this curriculum can't possibly cover all of the parables of Jesus, or all the events of his life, or even all of the events of Passion Week, in a single year. We assume that this curriculum is not your child's only exposure to the Bible. Your local church should provide your child's foundational education in the Gospel and Scripture. We are partnering with parents, teachers, and local churches to teach the Gospel message; this gives us the freedom to approach the curriculum the way we do.

During each year of the elementary curriculum, the lessons will repeat the nine categories, each year introducing new material and covering it in more depth. This means that a relatively short amount of time each year will be spent on the pivotal events of the Passion Week, Jesus' death, and the resurrection. We assume that your local church will play a major part in telling these stories and explaining their importance. However, it may seem a bit abrupt to end each year without looking in more detail at the crucifixion, resurrection, and post-resurrection appearances of Jesus. So we also offer a supplemental unit to make sure those topics are adequately covered during each year of Years One through Four.

Unit 1

Stories Jesus Told

For the Parent: Jesus was a master storyteller and preferred to use stories to introduce himself to his listeners. But this does not mean that the stories were easy to understand or that their meanings were self-evident. In fact, at times, Jesus seemed determined to obscure his message to those not prepared to hear it (Mark 4:11–12). Jesus revealed his message only to those who responded to him and followed him—to "insiders," so to speak. So, the parables are sometimes difficult to interpret. But they are also concrete and show up everywhere in the Gospels. Jesus liked talking in parables, and this is why we begin with them as we continue to introduce our children to his life and teachings.

<table>
<tr><td>

Lesson

1

</td><td align="right">

Matthew 21:28–32

Talking the Talk and Walking the Walk

</td></tr>
</table>

What the Parent Should Know: Jesus tells a parable of two sons who are asked by their father to work in the vineyard. The one says he will not work but then changes his mind and goes. The second son says he will work but then reneges. The first son obeys the father while the second does not join words and action. Jesus uses this parable to make a point about the hypocritical religious leaders of his day—their religious devotion is mere talk, but God requires more.

The parable is told in the temple courts (see v. 23) while Jesus is contending with the religious leaders (see vv. 23–27). The identity of the two sons reflects this confrontation. The son who reneges on his word to work the vineyard represents the religious leaders of the day who say all the right things but whose actions contradict their words. Throughout the Gospels, especially Matthew, Jesus chides the religious leaders for spiritual shallowness and hypocrisy, and this is another case. The other son represents the "tax collectors and prostitutes" (v. 31), those whom the religious leaders were quick to look down upon as "sinners" and therefore unworthy of the coming kingdom of God. Yet these are the ones who grasp Jesus' message—they believe Jesus and turn away from their sinful lives. Such action is required of all those who will be a part of the kingdom of God.

Entering the kingdom of God (or of heaven) does not mean earning one's way to heaven after death. The kingdom of God refers to the here-and-now kingdom that Jesus is building, where people know God intimately and act toward each other accordingly. This kingdom certainly extends to the life beyond, but throughout the Gospels Jesus typically has the here-and-now in his sights.

When Jesus says that tax collectors and sinners will enter this kingdom ahead of the religious leaders (v. 31), he is offending the latter's well-honed religious sensibilities. In Jesus' day, the common assumption was that becoming righteous by keeping the law was the key ingredient to ushering in God's kingdom. Jesus comes on the scene and not only personally announces the arrival of the kingdom but turns the tables on the religious leaders by challenging their expectations. He says that true "righteousness," and therefore membership in the kingdom, does not rest on adhering to the law. Rather, any sinner who repents and submits his will to Jesus and his message will gain entry.

Jesus reminds his hearers that repentance is the very message John the Baptist preached (see Matthew 3:2; see also Year One, Unit 8, Lesson 35). The religious elite should have learned their lesson, but instead they were deeply offended by John's announcement that even they, the keepers of the law, needed to repent like everyone else. Jesus furthers this offense by declaring that "sinners" who repent can enter the kingdom not only along with the religious elite but <u>ahead</u> of them.

The religious leaders still have not grasped the core of Jesus' message, that being part of the kingdom of God requires true repentance and turning one's life wholly over to God. This cannot be done from a safe distance as the religious leaders tried to do, merely by saying the right words and giving

       Lesson 1: Talking the Talk and Walking the Walk

*the appearance of godliness. Being a member of the kingdom of God is about
actions accompanying words, both talking the talk and walking the walk.*

*[Note: Jesus mentions tax collectors and prostitutes in this parable. These
two types of sinners were the scum of Jewish society: the latter needs no elabo-
ration, and the former were Jews who had sold out to collect taxes from the
Jews for the Roman overlords. In the lesson below, I refer to "tax collectors
and sinners," to keep the content at an age-appropriate level.]*

Begin by reading aloud:

> Then he told this parable: "What do you think? There was a man who
> had two sons. He went to the first and said, 'Son, go and work today
> in the vineyard.'
>
> " 'I will not,' he answered, but later he changed his mind and went.
>
> "Then the father went to the other son and said the same thing.
> He answered, 'I will, sir,' but he did not go.
>
> "Which of the two did what his father wanted?"
>
> "The first," they answered.
>
> Jesus said to them, "I tell you the truth, the tax collectors and
> the prostitutes are entering the kingdom of God ahead of you. For
> John came to you to show you the way of righteousness, and you did
> not believe him, but the tax collectors and the prostitutes did. And
> even after you saw this, you did not repent and believe him."

Jesus told a parable of a father, two sons, and a vineyard. (A vineyard
is where grapes are grown to make wine.) The father tells each son to go
work in the vineyard. The father expects both sons to do what he says.
The first son says "no" but later changes his mind and goes to work. The
second son says "yes" but doesn't go at all.

Jesus tells this parable to explain to the people that it is not enough
just to talk about God. Someone who really follows God will also do
what God wants. These two sons stand for two types of people Jesus
has in mind. The son who says "yes" but doesn't go is like some of the
religious leaders of Jesus' day, who talk about God a lot but do not obey
him. Jesus is angry with them because they should know better. Jesus
even reminds them that John the Baptist already told them they needed
to obey God, not just talk about him. (John the Baptist was Jesus' cousin
who went around the countryside telling people that Jesus was coming
and that everyone needed to listen to what Jesus says.)

The son who says "no" at first but then goes to work is like the tax
collectors and other sinners in Jesus' day. They disobey God at first but

then they change their minds and obey God. They say, "We want to leave behind our sinful life. We believe Jesus. We want to follow him and do what he says." These sinners understand that they must do what God wants, not just say they will.

Imagine that your mother tells you and your sister to straighten up your rooms. You say yes but then you sit down and watch TV. Your sister says no but then tells your mother she is sorry and spends hours cleaning up her room. So, which one of you is doing what your mother wants? The one who goes to her room and straightens it up, of course!

Doing what Jesus says is what counts with God, not just talking about God. That does not mean that God is watching you to make sure you are doing everything right, or that he will be angry if you make a mistake. God loves you and wants you to grow and to love him. We learn to know and love God when we try every day to do what God wants. For example, someone who says he loves God and then goes out and shows kindness to others is obeying God, not just talking about him. This is how we can grow to know God and love him.

<table>
<tr><td>Lesson
2</td><td>Mark 4:26–29
The Kingdom of God Grows
on its Own No Matter What</td></tr>
</table>

What the Parent Should Know: In this brief parable, the seed represents the spread of the kingdom of God as a result of Jesus' preaching—people hear, repent, and believe. Like the seed in this parable, the growth of the kingdom is relentless and inevitable. It cannot be stopped and its success does not depend on whether the seed is properly tended to by someone. And when the grain is fully ripe, it is harvested. This harvest may conjure up images of the Grim Reaper, but that is not what Jesus is talking about. The harvest is a symbolic description, telling us that the growth of the kingdom has reached full maturity. In an agricultural world, harvest represents growth, health, and life.

No one parable is meant to tell the whole story of the Gospel, and this parable is no exception. There are actually three seed parables in a row in Mark 4; and each paints a picture of the kingdom from a different angle. In the first, vv. 1–9, Jesus tells the parable of the sower (which he explains in vv. 13–20). There the seed is somewhat fragile; the quality of the soil determines whether the seed will grow to maturity. (We will look at this parable in Year Four.) But in our parable, the second of the three, the quality of the soil is irrelevant: the seeds spring up on their own regardless. Then in the third seed parable, in vv. 30–32, Jesus refers to the mustard seed (see Year One, Lesson 3). In that parable the growth of the kingdom is still in view, but the stress is on the surprising nature of the size of the kingdom from small beginnings.

In this parable, the emphasis is on the remarkable vigor and resiliency of the seed he has sown. The kingdom of God is not like a delicate seed, over which farmers fret whether it will yield its crop. It is robust, and certain to grow to full maturity without oversight. It is, after all, the kingdom of God. The harvest will come.

Begin by reading aloud:

In this parable, Jesus is teaching the people about what the kingdom of God is like. He says it is like seed that grows up from the ground. Here is what he says:

> "This is what the kingdom of God is like. A man scatters seed on the ground. Night and day, whether he sleeps or gets up, the seed sprouts and grows, though he does not know how. All by itself the soil produces grain—first the stalk, then the head, then the full kernel in the head. As soon as the grain is ripe, he puts the sickle to it, because the harvest has come."

Farmers don't just throw seeds anywhere and expect them to grow. They make sure the soil is healthy enough to give the seeds the nutrients they need to live and grow. They also don't just plant the seeds and forget about them. Farmers have to water them carefully every day. The same goes for you if you try to grow a seed in a pot in your house. You need to water it and care for it every day until it is strong.

Seeds need to be taken care of. But in this story, the seeds are scattered on the ground and grow tall and strong, even though no one is taking care of them. They just grow and grow and grow.

If you live near a city, you may have seen something unusual. In sidewalks, overpasses, and roads you will sometimes see grass and even trees growing up out of the cracks. How can that happen? Deep in those cracks is some soil. A single seed is carried by the wind and floats into a crack and sinks into the soil. The only water comes from the rain. No one takes care of that seed, but still you have a tall and strong tree growing out of the crack in the cement.

Jesus tells this story to teach the people about the kingdom of God. This kingdom is not made up of armies and castles. It is made up of people who love God and follow what Jesus teaches about God. Jesus says that the kingdom of God grows like this seed that was scattered on the ground. Those seeds grow and grow no matter what. Nothing can stop them from growing. Just like the seeds, wherever Jesus went and talked about God, people kept coming from all over to listen. More and more people followed Jesus. The kingdom of God kept getting bigger and bigger. Nothing could stop it.

Today, the kingdom of God is still growing, and nothing can stop it. All over the world are people who love God and follow Jesus every day. No one has to stand watch to make sure that God's kingdom keeps growing. This is God's kingdom, and he makes sure it continues to grow no matter what.

<table>
<tr><td>Lesson
3</td><td>Luke 10:30–37</td></tr>
</table>

Everyone is Your Neighbor

What the Parent Should Know: This is one of the best-known and loved parables of Jesus. Jesus told the parable in response to a question posed to him by an "expert in the Law" (v. 25). The expert wanted to know how to inherit eternal life, which was a common question; he probably asked it to see what kind of teacher Jesus was. Jesus responded by putting the ball back in his court: "What is written in the Law?" The expert answered that one must love God fully and unconditionally, and love one's neighbor (which is a perfectly acceptable answer; Jesus says something similar in Matthew 22:37–40; see also Deuteronomy 6:5 and Leviticus 19:18).

But the expert in the Law wanted to corner Jesus into a sparring contest about interpretation (which is what "he wanted to justify himself" means in v. 29—he wanted to look good). So he asked Jesus, "Fine, but what does 'neighbor' mean? What are the sorts of people I am called upon to love?"

Jesus' answer is the parable, and no expert in the Law could have anticipated what Jesus was about to say. By making a Samaritan the center of the story, Jesus is saying that your neighbors are not just people who are part of your group, but people outside of your group—even people you hate.

                    Lesson 3: Everyone is Your Neighbor

We might not think much of this today, but in Jesus' day, thinking of Samaritans as neighbors was very troublesome for observant Jews such as this expert in the Law. There are two reasons for this.

First, Jews hated Samaritans for historical reasons. Samaritans claimed to be the true descendents of the northern kingdom of Israel that was sent into exile by the Assyrians in 722 BC. They also claimed that the holy mountain was Mount Gerizim, not Mount Sinai (Deuteronomy 11:29 mentions Mount Gerizim as the place from which the Israelites would be blessed by God). Mainstream Jews, however, considered the Samaritans to have co-mingled with Gentiles after the Assyrian invasion, thus forfeiting their status as pure Israelites. These long-standing tensions were very much alive in Jesus' day. (See also John 4:1–42 and the story of the Samaritan woman at the well.)

Second, even though in the Old Testament there is compassion for non-Israelites (for example, Exodus 22:21), the command to love one's neighbor is directed specifically toward fellow Israelites (Leviticus 19:18). Outsiders were largely thought of as a threat to Israel. This kind of hostility had increased in Jesus' day, with the various political and religious tensions introduced by first Greek and then Roman occupation. These tensions make Jesus' parable all the more striking. (Jesus captured this same sentiment in Matthew 5:43-44, where he said to love one's enemies, not just one's neighbor.) An enemy was not simply an individual you didn't like, but an ethnic entity.

With that in mind, we can see the impact of this parable. First a priest and then a Levite step around a beaten man, feeling no obligation to come to his aid. "Priests and Levites" are two different classes of priests and together represent the religious authorities. Priests were descendents of Aaron, Moses' brother, the chosen line from within the tribe of Levi in charge of the tabernacle and later the temple. All other descendents of the tribe of Levi were called Levites and were given lesser duties in the temple; they were in effect helpers to the priests.

But the hated Samaritan sees the man lying there, and without asking questions about who he is—whether Jew, Samaritan, Greek, Roman, whatever—he helps him. The Samaritan, of all people, acts like a neighbor toward the man who needs help, the very thing the priest and Levite failed to do.

Jesus' challenge to the expert in the Law is clear: "You want to know what God requires? You want to know who your neighbor is? Let this <u>Samaritan</u> teach you. Watch <u>him</u> be a neighbor to the person who crosses his path." "Neighbor" now extends to even one's sworn enemies. In fact, a Samaritan enemy is more like God than this supposed "expert" in the Law.

Members of the kingdom, Jesus preached, are called to love God fully and to love all people—which means old hostilities between Jews and Gentiles are to be obliterated. Whoever is to be a member of Jesus' kingdom must see himself as a neighbor to everyone.

Begin by reading aloud:

Today's story from the Gospels is one that Jesus tells to a man who comes to talk to him. This man is an expert in the Jewish Law, and he comes to visit Jesus so that he can ask, "What do I have to do to inherit eternal life?"

Jesus reminds him of how the Law answers that question: you must love God and your neighbor. But the expert wants to know, "Who is my neighbor?" He wants to know what kind of people he has to be kind to. To explain who a "neighbor" is, Jesus tells a story about a Samaritan.

You should know that Samaritans and Jews were enemies back then. They had been enemies for hundreds of years. Each nation thought it was closer to God than the other. In Jesus' day, Jews looked down on Samaritans. Jews would try to avoid being around Samaritans or even speaking to them.

So, Jesus tells a story about a good Samaritan to show that a neighbor is not someone who lives next door to you, and not just someone you like. A neighbor is anyone in need, even someone you think you should hate.

> "A man was going down from Jerusalem to Jericho, when he fell into the hands of robbers. They stripped him of his clothes, beat him, and went away, leaving him half dead. A priest happened to be going down the same road, and when he saw the man, he passed by on the other side. So too, a Levite, when he came to the place and saw him, passed by on the other side. But a Samaritan, as he traveled, came where the man was; and when he saw him, he took pity on him. He went to him and bandaged his wounds, pouring on oil and wine. Then he put the man on his own donkey, took him to an inn, and took care of him. The next day he took out two silver coins and gave them to the innkeeper. 'Look after him,' he said, 'and when I return, I will reimburse you for any extra expense you may have.'
>
> "Which of these three do you think was a neighbor to the man who fell into the hands of robbers?"
>
> The expert in the law replied, "The one who had mercy on him."
>
> Jesus told him, "Go and do likewise."

In this story, a man is walking along a rocky road from Jerusalem to the town of Jericho. That is a long walk (17 miles), and there are plenty

Lesson 3: Everyone is Your Neighbor

of places for robbers to hide and jump out and rob people. Sure enough, this man is robbed and beaten so badly he almost dies.

Two Jewish leaders, a priest and a Levite (priests took care of the temple and Levites were their helpers), come along and find him. Even though the man is almost dead, they just keep on walking. They should have stopped to help him. This is what God would want them to do, because in the kingdom of God people are supposed to love each other the way God does.

Along comes a Samaritan, a hated enemy of the Jews. He stops and helps the beaten man. He bandages the man's wounds, takes him to an inn (there were no hospitals back then), and gives the innkeeper money to give the beaten man anything he needs to get better. The Samaritan even promises to come back and pay more if needed.

Jesus tells this story to show that members of God's kingdom are those who are kind to others, even going out of their way to be kind if that is what it takes. Some of the religious leaders thought the kingdom was only for them and their fellow Jews—and especially not for the hated Samaritans—but they were wrong. Jesus shows that the kingdom of God is open to everyone who wants to follow God, no matter where they are from.

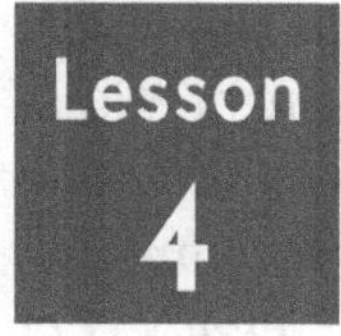

Lesson 4

Matthew 18:21–35

Don't Stop Forgiving Others

What the Parent Should Know: Peter approaches Jesus to ask him how many times he should forgive a brother who sins against him. Peter suggests "seven times" (v. 21), and he is hardly being stingy, for the Jewish custom was to forgive as much as three times. By going beyond the custom, Peter likely assumed he would receive Jesus' approval. But Jesus answers famously, "Not seven times, but seventy times seven" (or "seventy-seven times"—the Greek can be read either way). Of course, this number is not to be taken literally. Jesus means, "Don't stop forgiving."

In this parable, the sin in view is not a life-threatening situation between the powerful and powerless, such as emotional or physical abuse. So, this parable should not be read as commanding the weak and oppressed to suffer mistreatment. It has to do with social and personal relationships between people, where one party does some harm to the other.

As the story goes, a servant owes a considerable sum of 10,000 talents to a king. One talent was worth 60 minas, and one mina was about a hundred days' wage for a worker. So, one talent was worth about 6,000 days' wage, or about 16 ½ years. Ten thousand talents is therefore an astronomical sum, and is probably more or less equivalent to how we use "a bazillion dollars" to indicate a ridiculously large amount of money. The sum simply cannot be paid, so the king threatens to sell him and his family into slavery, along with his belongings to repay it. And before we are too hard on this king, his act was accepted practice, even hinted at in the Old Testament (2 Kings 4:1).

The servant begs for the king's patience, which is almost comical, since there is no hope of paying the king back—this would be like asking a factory worker to pay off the national debt ("Give me some time, I'll do it"). Still, the king forgives the debt entirely, an incalculable display of forgiveness and mercy.

But the servant also has someone in his debt. Someone owes him "a hundred denarii"—one denarius was about a day's wage for a laborer. So 100 denarii is no small amount for a worker, although still in the realm of reality. The man begs for patience, too, but the forgiven servant is deaf to his pleas and has him thrown into prison. The king hears of it, and turns the servant over to be tortured.

This parable is a concrete illustration of why followers of Jesus are to display limitless forgiveness. As we see elsewhere in the New Testament, sin is understood as a debt the offender owes to the offended. (Jesus uses the same idea in the Lord's Prayer, Matthew 6:12.) Our debt to God is astronomical, and only his boundless forgiveness can pay it. We who are now members of the kingdom of God must reflect that same mercy to those whose debt to us is laughably small by comparison—free, limitless forgiveness. Failure to forgive another is unthinkable to someone who claims to believe in a God who forgives so generously.

Begin by reading aloud:

Peter came to Jesus and asked, "Lord, how many times shall I forgive my brother when he sins against me? Up to seven times?"

Jesus answered, "I tell you, not seven times, but seventy-seven times.

"Therefore, the kingdom of heaven is like a king who wanted to settle accounts with his servants. As he began the settlement, a man who owed him ten thousand talents was brought to him. Since he was not able to pay, the master ordered that he and his wife and his children and all that he had be sold to repay the debt.

"The servant fell on his knees before him. 'Be patient with me,' he begged, 'and I will pay back everything.' The servant's master took pity on him, canceled the debt, and let him go.

"But when that servant went out, he found one of his fellow servants who owed him a hundred denarii. He grabbed him and began to choke him. 'Pay back what you owe me!' he demanded.

"His fellow servant fell to his knees and begged him, 'Be patient with me, and I will pay you back.'

"But he refused. Instead, he went off and had the man thrown into prison until he could pay the debt. When the other servants saw what had happened, they were greatly distressed and went and told their master everything that had happened.

"Then the master called the servant in. 'You wicked servant,' he said, 'I canceled all that debt of yours because you begged me to. Shouldn't you have had mercy on your fellow servant just as I had on you?' In anger his master turned him over to the jailers to be tortured, until he should pay back all he owed.

"This is how my heavenly Father will treat each of you unless you forgive your brother from your heart."

Peter comes up to Jesus and asks him how many times he needs to forgive someone who does something wrong to him. Peter asks if seven times is enough. If you think about it, seven times is a lot. What if your brother or sister took your favorite shirt and cut it up with a pair of scissors, and then asked you for forgiveness? You should forgive them when they ask. But what if they do something else to you . . . and then something else, again . . . and again . . . and again . . . and again . . . and again . . . and again—six more times in all? It would be very hard to forgive that many times.

But Jesus doesn't say to Peter that seven times is good enough. He says "seventy times seven." That doesn't mean that you should multiply and come up with 490. That is Jesus' way of saying that we should *always* be ready to forgive others when they sincerely ask to be forgiven.

Why does Jesus say we should always be ready to forgive? Because God is always ready to forgive us. So, Jesus tells this story about a king and his servant to explain how we are to forgive. The servant owes the king 10,000 talents. Just one talent was a lot of money back then—about as much money as a worker would make in sixteen years! So 10,000 talents is like Jesus saying, "The servant owed like a bazillion dollars!" It is much, much more than a servant could ever hope to pay back. He would have to work for 160,000 years to earn that much money!

Instead of making the servant pay it back, the king forgives the debt. That means the man won't be thrown into prison, and his wife and children won't be sold into slavery either (which is something kings did back then if they did not get paid back). The king had great mercy on his servant.

The servant is so relieved that he has been forgiven. But what does he do? He goes out and finds someone who owes him a lot less money—a hundred denarii. One denarius was a Roman silver coin worth about one day's payment for a worker. He couldn't pay it back, so the servant had him thrown into prison. When the king hears about this, he throws the servant into prison to be tortured.

The servant had been forgiven a lot by the king—more than he could count. But he could not forgive someone else even a little bit.

Jesus is saying that God forgives us again and again, more than we can count. Whenever we do something to hurt others—like speaking angrily or making fun of them—we need God's forgiveness. And if we think about it, we do and say things probably every day that hurt others. But God is always ready to forgive us.

In this story, Jesus is teaching us to always be ready to forgive others, just the way God is always ready to forgive us. When we forgive others, we know that God is truly living in our hearts, because we will be acting toward others the way God acts toward us. And when we forgive others, we are also giving them a taste for how much God is ready to forgive them, too.

Matthew 20:1–16

God is Equally Gracious to All

What the Parent Should Know: In this parable, Jesus says that the kingdom of heaven is like a landowner who goes out and hires workers for the vineyard. In order to understand Jesus' meaning, we must keep in mind that the kingdom of heaven is not the afterlife. As we have seen in the other parables in this section, it refers to the here-and-now reality of King Jesus creating a new kingdom on earth where people know God and follow him with their whole hearts.

The point of this parable is that all God's workers are to serve him with gratitude for his grace and without any feeling of superiority toward other workers. What creates the tension in the parable is that the landowner decides to pay all workers the equal amount (one denarius, a full day's wage) regardless of when they were hired during the day. That should strike us as unfair, as it did those in Jesus' day. It is only natural for any worker to feel mistreated when a newly hired person receives the same wage. (A modern parallel might be for a newly hired worker to be paid the same hourly wage as someone who has been working faithfully for years.)

Jesus drives the point home in the last verse: "So the last will be first, and the first will be last" (20:16; Jesus makes a similar point in 19:16–30). Jesus does not mean that first and last will switch places—as if the first, who think they are all high and mighty, will be put in their place, and the ones called last will be given some priority. He means that God treats the first and the last equally, as he does the workers in this parable. This is an act of grace on God's part. Therefore, those who have labored longer, rather than being envious and jockeying for position, should rejoice at the landowner's generosity.

Yes, this is "unfair" but that is precisely the point of this parable and all other parables. The stories Jesus tells are meant to leave people scratching their heads. Jesus aims to turn upside down conventional ways of thinking about how the world works. Sinners and religious leaders are of equal status in the kingdom (Lesson 1), as are Jews and Samaritans (Lesson 3). In this parable we learn that there is no seniority structure in the kingdom of heaven either. Such a structure might have meant something in Jewish or Roman culture—as well as our contemporary culture—but not for followers of Jesus.

Begin by reading aloud:

Jesus tells his disciples a story about a landowner who hires people to work the land. This is what he says:

> "The kingdom of heaven is like a landowner who went out early in the morning to hire men to work in his vineyard. He agreed to pay them a denarius for the day and sent them into his vineyard.
>
> "About the third hour he went out and saw others standing in the marketplace doing nothing. He told them, 'You also go and work in my vineyard, and I will pay you whatever is right.' So they went.

"He went out again about the sixth hour and the ninth hour and did the same thing. About the eleventh hour he went out and found still others standing around. He asked them, 'Why have you been standing here all day long doing nothing?'

" 'Because no one has hired us,' they answered.

"He said to them, 'You also go and work in my vineyard.'

"When evening came, the owner of the vineyard said to his foreman, 'Call the workers and pay them their wages, beginning with the last ones hired and going on to the first.'

"The workers who were hired about the eleventh hour came and each received a denarius. So when those came who were hired first, they expected to receive more. But each one of them also received a denarius. When they received it, they began to grumble against the landowner. 'These men who were hired last worked only one hour,' they said, 'and you have made them equal to us who have borne the burden of the work and the heat of the day.'

"But he answered one of them, 'Friend, I am not being unfair to you. Didn't you agree to work for a denarius? Take your pay and go. I want to give the man who was hired last the same as I gave you. Don't I have the right to do what I want with my own money? Or are you envious because I am generous?'

"So the last will be first, and the first will be last."

The landowner in this story hires people to work in the vineyard. He hires the people at different times in the day. At the end of the day when he hands out the money, he does something that seems unfair. He pays everyone exactly the same amount of money, no matter how long they worked that day. The workers who were hired first complain that it isn't fair. They should be paid more because they worked longer.

What if your mother wakes you up early on a Saturday and tells you, "It is 8:00. I have jobs for you to do around the house all day until 5:00. It is a lot of work, but when you are done at the end of the day, we will go to the toy store and you can pick out any toy worth $50." Well, that sounds just great to you. So, you jump out of bed, work hard all day, and wait for that trip to the toy store.

Your little brother sleeps in and gets up at 10:00. Your mother gives him the same deal: work the rest of the day and you can pick out a $50 toy. You might feel angry with your mother and your brother. It isn't fair. And just when you're thinking about how angry you are, your mother does the same thing later in the day, again and again and again: she hires your sister at noon, and then later another kid down the street at 2:00, and then someone else at 4:00 who only works for an hour. You worked all day, nine hours, but you all get the same pay: a $50 toy.

That seems very unfair, doesn't it? This is what some of Jesus' followers were complaining about. They had been with Jesus since the beginning. They had left everything they had to follow him. Now more and more people were following Jesus, and the disciples began to think, "Hey, I've been here longer. How come Jesus treats us all like we are equals?"

Jesus tells stories like this to show us that his kingdom has different rules from what we are used to. Sure, if your mother really gave everyone a $50 toy, it would be unfair. But Jesus uses a story like the one about the landowner to teach us that in God's kingdom, God treats everyone the same. Why does God do this? Because God loves us all the same. He does not love others more because they have been followers of Jesus for a longer time. Just like the workers in this story, whoever comes to Jesus and says, "I want to work in God's kingdom," is treated the same by God.

Miracles Jesus Did

For the Parent: Jesus' miracles were another means of introducing himself to the people of his time. They were not, however, merely displays of strength or power, intended to draw attention to himself. And the miracles did not "prove" that Jesus was divine. (Similar abilities were displayed by Moses and Elijah, for example.)

Rather, by performing miracles, Jesus was drawing attention to his role as God's special servant. He was demonstrating that his "connection" with God was indeed unique and that he was, therefore, sent by God to do his work. The miracles established in the eyes of the people (and the disciples, see John 2:11 in Year One, Lesson 6) that Jesus had God's authority behind him, which is why John refers to them as "signs" (v. 11). As we see so often in the Gospels, Jesus' authority was the very thing that the religious leaders kept challenging.

Jesus' miracles can be understood from two angles. First, miracles show Jesus' control over the powers of creation. When Jesus controls wind and water, heals the sick, and raises the dead, he is showing his ability to manipulate the forces of creation, just as Yahweh, the Father God and Creator, does in the Old Testament. These miracles display the intimacy between the Father and Son, and so express what is said succinctly in Colossians 1:16: "All things were created by him and for him."

Second, healings are part of the Old Testament picture of the coming messiah. A "messiah" in the Old Testament was someone who was "anointed" (this is what the Hebrew word means), or chosen, to be a representative of God in some respect. Typically, the messianic role was one fulfilled by kings: they were all anointed with oil to rule the people for God. So performing miracles was a part of Jesus' messianic role—he was representing God to the people. We see this, for example, in Jesus' response to John the Baptist's question in Luke 7:22 and in Old Testament passages such as Isaiah 35:3–6. The miracles are loud exclamations that the kingdom of God, hinted at in various portions of the Old Testament, had indeed arrived in the person of Jesus.

<table>
<tr><td>

Lesson

6

</td><td>

Matthew 17:24–27

Kings Don't Pay Taxes

</td></tr>
</table>

What the Parent Should Know: The Old Testament required every male twenty years old or more to pay an annual tax to the temple (actually, it began as a tabernacle tax in Exodus 30:11–16 and then morphed to a temple tax, as we see in Nehemiah 10:32 and 2 Chronicles 24:8–10). The amount was fairly small, a half shekel, which equaled two drachmas (about two days' wages). This tax was needed to maintain the temple and the sacrificial system.

In this story, Jesus and his disciples have just arrived at Capernaum from Galilee, and the temple tax collectors want to see whether Jesus will meet his biblical obligation. These tax collectors are not those we meet elsewhere, who collect taxes for the Romans and are counted among the "sinners" (e.g., Year One Lesson 4, Luke 18:10–14). These are Jewish officials charged to make sure funds come in to maintain the temple. By this time in Jesus' ministry, the religious leaders have had enough of Jesus' challenges to their authority. Showing Jesus to be disloyal to the temple, and therefore to Judaism, would help them build a case against him and make it easier to get rid of him.

That is why the temple tax collectors approach Peter to ask whether Jesus in fact pays the tax. Peter answers with a simple yes, but in private Jesus takes the matter a step further. Jesus says that it is good to pay the tax, but only so as not to "offend" the tax collectors. Of course, Jesus is hardly concerned about upsetting them: he's been upsetting people all along. He simply means that he does not want to give them an excuse to have him arrested—not yet.

Jesus then explains himself to Peter. Jesus is exempt from paying the tax because he is the Son of God, the king of Israel, who is worshiped in the temple. This makes Jesus royalty. He is the final, ultimate, long-expected king of Israel who has come to deliver his people. Such a son does not pay the temple tax.

The fish with the coin in its mouth is likely what will grab a child's attention, but the fish has no hidden meaning. Peter was a fisherman, they were in Capernaum by the Sea of Galilee, and fish were plentiful. The main point here is not "why a fish?" nor even how the coin got there (maybe the fish gobbled up a shiny coin from the bottom of the lake). Getting money from the fish's mouth is Jesus' way of paying the tax so as not to offend, while at the same time not paying it out of his own pocket, since he is royalty and is therefore exempt from paying it. If Jesus had paid the tax in a conventional manner, he would have denied his own royal status.

Jesus is royalty, the son of the king; but for now, this is something he wanted only his disciples to hear.

Begin by reading aloud:

> After Jesus and his disciples arrived in Capernaum, the collectors of the two-drachma tax came to Peter and asked, "Doesn't your teacher pay the temple tax?"
>
> "Yes, he does," he replied.
>
> When Peter came into the house, Jesus was the first to speak. "What do you think, Simon?" he asked. "From whom do the kings of the earth collect duty and taxes—from their own sons or from others?"
>
> "From others," Peter answered.
>
> "Then the sons are exempt," Jesus said to him. "But so that we may not offend them, go to the lake and throw out your line. Take the first fish you catch; open its mouth and you will find a four-drachma coin. Take it and give it to them for my tax and yours."

Finding a coin in a fish's mouth sounds like the most interesting and important part of the story, doesn't it? Wouldn't you like to find money by catching fish and opening their mouths? But the main point of this story is not finding money in a fish's mouth. The main point is that Jesus is the Son of God.

In the Old Testament, the Israelites had to pay a tax every year so that the temple could keep running. The priests needed money to buy animals to sacrifice and repair the building. Hundreds of years later, in Jesus' time, once a year each Jewish man paid two drachmas for the temple tax, about what a worker would get for two days' work. Temple tax collectors made sure that the temple tax was paid. The tax was like tithing is in churches today. Tithing means giving a portion of your money to the church each week. If people didn't tithe, the pastors couldn't make a living and the church's bills wouldn't get paid.

In this story, the tax collectors ask Peter whether Jesus pays the temple tax. They ask Peter because they are trying to trap Jesus. They are angry with Jesus because he has been criticizing the priests and the teachers of the law for a long time. Jesus has been telling the people that the leaders don't really know God and they should listen to him instead. They hope that Peter will say, "No, Jesus does not pay the temple tax." Not paying the tax is against the law, and so they could finally have Jesus arrested and get even with him.

Jesus does pay the temple tax, but he wants Peter to understand something. Jesus tells Peter that he does not *have* to pay the tax. The reason Jesus does not have to pay the tax is because the temple is God's house, and Jesus is God's Son. Sons don't pay taxes to their fathers, and so Jesus does not have to pay the temple tax.

Why then does Jesus pay the tax anyway, even though he is God's Son and doesn't have to? Jesus pays the tax because he knows the tax collectors are trying to trap him so they can arrest him. Jesus is not afraid of being arrested, but now is not the time for that. Jesus still has more to teach the people before he is arrested and crucified.

So, Jesus pays the temple tax to keep from being arrested right then and there. But he doesn't pay it out of his own pocket like everyone else. If he did that, he wouldn't be showing that he was the Son of God. So he doesn't reach into his pocket and pull out a two-drachma coin. He has another idea. He tells Peter to catch a fish and take the coin from the fish's mouth. That way Jesus still pays the temple tax without paying for it himself.

The tax collectors think Jesus should have to pay the temple tax, but they are wrong. They do not understand that Jesus is the Son of God. But Jesus loves his disciples and explains to them that he is God's Son.

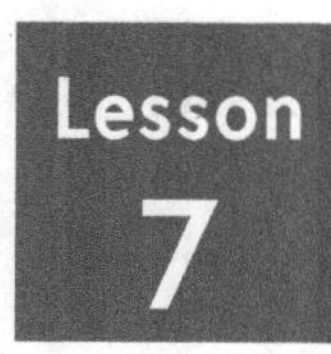

John 4:46–54

Taking Jesus at His Word

What the Parent Should Know: When this story begins, Jesus has just arrived in Cana in Galilee, the site of his first miracle in John's Gospel, where he turned water to wine at the wedding (John 2:1–11, Year One, Lesson 6). He is greeted with enthusiasm by the crowd, for they have heard of his powers and are no doubt curious as to what Jesus will do next. They are looking for a performance. Instead Jesus utters a simple healing word that can only be verified by a frightened but trusting father.

The man who comes to him is a royal official in the service of Herod Antipas (ruler of Galilee and one of the sons of Herod the Great). His son is close to death, twenty miles away in Capernaum. The official has come all that way to beg Jesus to heal his son.

The heart of the story is that Jesus heals the boy from a distance, without immediate proof, and that the official trusts him at once. The people are looking for some entertainment from this traveling healer. Jesus knows exactly what they are thinking and chides them: "Unless you people see miraculous signs and wonders you will never believe" (v. 48). In other words, "All you people care about is miracles, and you want to see them with your own eyes before you trust me."

But the official "takes Jesus at his word" (v. 50), and travels home to find his son has been healed at the exact time Jesus uttered the healing word. As a result the official and his household believe in Jesus.

The trust shown by the officer of the hated Herod exposes the lack of faith of the residents of his own hometown—people who knew Jesus and should have known better. It would have been easy for Jesus to oblige the curiosity of the Galileans and so perhaps gain a stronger following. Instead, Jesus sends a very different message: "My miracles are not for entertainment value, nor are they an end in themselves. I am not seeking your acclaim. I am showing you who I am and that I am worthy of your trust."

Begin by reading aloud:

> Once more he visited Cana in Galilee, where he had turned the water into wine. And there was a certain royal official whose son lay sick at Capernaum. When this man heard that Jesus had arrived in Galilee

from Judea, he went to him and begged him to come and heal his son, who was close to death.

"Unless you people see miraculous signs and wonders," Jesus told him, "you will never believe."

The royal official said, "Sir, come down before my child dies."

Jesus replied, "You may go. Your son will live."

The man took Jesus at his word and departed. While he was still on the way, his servants met him with the news that his boy was living. When he inquired as to the time when his son got better, they said to him, "The fever left him yesterday at the seventh hour."

Then the father realized that this was the exact time at which Jesus had said to him, "Your son will live." So he and all his household believed.

This was the second miraculous sign that Jesus performed, having come from Judea to Galilee.

When this story begins, Jesus has just arrived at the city of Cana. Cana was in Galilee, and Galilee was where Jesus grew up. Everyone in Galilee knows about Jesus. And Jesus has already done one miracle in Cana—he turned water into wine at a wedding. So the people of Cana know about Jesus' miracles. They all come out to see the next miracle Jesus will do. They are curious.

Then a man comes up to Jesus—a man who is an officer of King Herod. The Romans made Herod king over the Jews, so Herod works for the Roman emperor. The Jews don't like being controlled by the Romans— and they hate King Herod, because he is helping the Romans. They also hate Herod's officers, so this man is not very well liked by the crowd!

This officer is not even from Jesus' hometown Galilee, but from Capernaum, twenty miles away. He does not know Jesus like the Galileans do. He comes all that way to see Jesus because his son is very sick and almost dead. Unlike the people of Galilee, the officer is not just curious. He needs Jesus' help, so he begs Jesus to heal his son.

Jesus does—but he doesn't go all the way to Capernaum to heal the boy. He just tells the officer that the boy is healed, right then and there.

As an army officer, the man could have ordered Jesus to come home with him to make sure the boy is actually healed. But instead, the officer trusts Jesus. The officer does not need to see any proof that the boy is healed. He takes Jesus at his word. So he goes home and finds that his son is indeed healed. And then everyone in his house comes to trust Jesus, too.

The people of Jesus' hometown do not take Jesus at his word. They want to see Jesus do a miracle before their eyes. But the officer, someone who doesn't know Jesus like the others do, trusts Jesus. He doesn't need to see the miracle. He only needs to hear Jesus say, "Your boy is healed" and he trusts him right away.

Jesus heals the boy to teach the people of his hometown that they need to trust what he says without seeing a miracle. Jesus is telling them that they can take him at his word, just like the officer did, because Jesus is trustworthy.

<table>
<tr><td>Lesson
8</td><td>Luke 18:35–43
King Jesus Has Mercy
on the Helpless</td></tr>
</table>

What the Parent Should Know: A blind beggar, sitting along the road to Jeri-cho, is told that Jesus is passing by. He calls out to Jesus not once but twice, asking Jesus to be merciful to him. Jesus shows mercy by healing the lowly and helpless man. Some kings are tyrants, and others are too busy with more important matters. But King Jesus has mercy on the helpless.

The beggar refers to Jesus by the royal title Son of David, which suggests that the beggar is a Jew and sees Jesus as Israel's king. In the Old Testament, Israel hoped for a future king to come and deliver them from foreign oppression and then guide them in faithfulness to the law. They spoke of this hoped-for king not only as a military figure, but as someone who would heal the blind and preach good news to the poor (e.g., Isaiah 29:18–21; 35:5–6; 61:1). This was likely symbolic language in the Old Testament, where Israel's spiritual blindness would be healed. But Jesus did physically what was meant symbolically in the Old Testament.

By healing those in need, Jesus shows that he is the hoped-for Messiah, the Old Testament future king. Earlier in Luke, Jesus made this same point to the disciples of John the Baptist. John was in prison and wondered whether Jesus was the Messiah. Jesus told John's disciples to go back to John and report: "The blind receive sight . . . and good news is preached to the poor" (Luke 7:22; see also 4:18). By his healings, Jesus shows that the Messiah has now come.

So, the mercy Jesus shows to the blind beggar is not a random act of kind-ness on the way to Calvary but a concrete demonstration to those with eyes to see that the kingdom of God has come. The Gospels emphasize again and again that, as the Messiah, Jesus is merciful to those on the fringes of society: a tax collector or prostitute who needs forgiveness, a widow with no means of sustaining herself, or the lame and sick, who rely wholly on the kindness of strangers to live day to day.

The beggar's shouts irritate those in the crowd (v. 39); they do not see that the beggar's shouts are announcing the messiah's presence. Although blind, this beggar has 20/20 spiritual vision. Amid a crowd of ardent followers of Jesus, the blind beggar alone sees Jesus for what he is—the Son of David, here to show mercy.

Begin by reading aloud:

> As Jesus approached Jericho, a blind man was sitting by the roadside begging. When he heard the crowd going by, he asked what was happening. They told him, "Jesus of Nazareth is passing by."
>
> He called out, "Jesus, Son of David, have mercy on me!"
>
> Those who led the way rebuked him and told him to be quiet, but he shouted all the more, "Son of David, have mercy on me!"
>
> Jesus stopped and ordered the man to be brought to him. When he came near, Jesus asked him, "What do you want me to do for you?"
>
> "Lord, I want to see," he replied.
>
> Jesus said to him, "Receive your sight; your faith has healed you." Immediately he received his sight and followed Jesus, praising God. When all the people saw it, they also praised God.

In this story, Jesus is on the road to Jericho with a large crowd surrounding him. A blind man hears all the noise and wants to know what is going on. He is told that Jesus is passing by. The blind beggar begins to shout to Jesus to have mercy on him. Mercy means helping someone who can't help himself.

If you go into big cities today, you will often see people begging for money or food. Many of these people have no homes to go to; they live on the streets or in shelters. Some of those who beg can't walk or see. They have no way of buying what they need. They can only depend on others to help them. They hope for strangers passing by to give them money to buy food and clothing.

In Jesus' day, things were pretty much the same. If someone was blind, couldn't walk, or was very sick, he would not be able to work for

　　　　　　　Lesson 8: King Jesus Has Mercy on the Helpless

himself. He would have to rely completely on the kindness of people passing by to give him some money or food. And there were no shelters or soup kitchens for these helpless, homeless people!

So, the blind man begs Jesus for mercy—but not for food or shelter. The blind beggar wants to be healed and he knows Jesus can do it. (He probably has heard the stories of Jesus healing other people.) Some people in the crowd think the blind man is bothering Jesus—maybe even embarrassing him. After all, Jesus is the Son of David. David was Israel's most powerful and famous king in the Old Testament. To be called Son of David meant that people thought you were their new king.

The crowd thinks that Jesus is too famous and important to be bothered by beggars. They tell the beggar to keep quiet, but he keeps on shouting. But Jesus is not the kind of king that ignores beggars or looks down on them like people expect a king to do. Jesus stops, asks the beggar what he can do for him, and then heals him.

Now the blind man can see. He is so full of joy that he follows Jesus around, praising and thanking God because he can see. Everyone else starts praising God, too. The crowd did not want Jesus to bother with the blind beggar, but now they understand. Jesus is the king, the Son of David, and this king has mercy on those who can't help themselves.

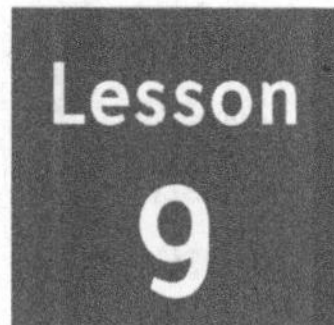

Lesson 9

Luke 17:11–19

The Faith of the Outsiders

What the Parent Should Know: As the story begins, Jesus is on his way to Jerusalem. He knows that death waits for him there, but that does not deter him from fulfilling one key aspect of his role as messiah: to help the helpless (see Lesson 8, also Luke 7:22), even if one of the helpless is a Samaritan, a people despised by the Jews.

In this story, the helpless are ten lepers. "Leprosy" is the English word used for a variety of infectious skin diseases in the Bible; it is not the same as "leprosy" in the modern sense (Hansen's disease). Nevertheless, leprosy made someone a complete outsider, not only because the condition was contagious but because it meant the leper was ritually unclean (see Leviticus 13–14). Lepers were unable to maintain contact with anyone other than fellow lepers, which made begging even more difficult. Lepers were the most destitute and pitiful group in the ancient world.

These lepers see Jesus coming, and keeping their distance, they shout to Jesus as master and ask him for pity (v. 13)—meaning, like the blind beggar in Lesson 8, they were pleading with Jesus to show them mercy and heal them.

Jesus does not pronounce healing. He simply tells them to show themselves to the priests. According to the Old Testament, lepers are supposed to show themselves to priests <u>after</u> they have been cleansed to verify the fact (Leviticus 13:19; 14:1–11). By telling the lepers to go to the priest before there was any evidence of healing, Jesus is saying, "Rest assured, you are as good as healed." And sure enough, all ten are healed once they have started on the way to see the priest. (We see a similar scene in Lesson 7, where Jesus tells the Roman official to return home before he sees any evidence that his son is healed.)

Once healed, the nine Jewish lepers continue on to fulfill their Old Testament obligation. On one level this is understandable: they are obeying the law. On the other hand, by failing to stop dead in their tracks and think about what just happened to them, they show a lack of perception about who Jesus is.

A common theme in the Gospels is that Jesus' message is for the disenfranchised and "foreigners" (see v. 18) as well as the Jews. Further, these "outsiders" often recognize Israel's messiah more quickly than the Jews themselves do. This miracle story illustrates that theme: all ten lepers are healed, but the nine Jewish lepers do not acknowledge Jesus. Only the Samaritan comes and throws himself at Jesus' feet. So this lesson not only shows Jesus' care for the disenfranchised and the need for people to trust him, but also shows that those on the outside may be quicker to recognize that Jesus is the Son of God.

Begin by reading aloud:

> Now on his way to Jerusalem, Jesus traveled along the border between Samaria and Galilee. As he was going into a village, ten men who had leprosy met him. They stood at a distance and called out in a loud voice, "Jesus, Master, have pity on us!"
>
> When he saw them, he said, "Go, show yourselves to the priests." And as they went, they were cleansed.
>
> One of them, when he saw he was healed, came back, praising God in a loud voice. He threw himself at Jesus' feet and thanked him—and he was a Samaritan.
>
> Jesus asked, "Were not all ten cleansed? Where are the other nine? Was no one found to return and give praise to God except this

Lesson 9: The Faith of the Outsiders

foreigner?" Then he said to him, "Rise and go; your faith has made you well."

Jesus is on his way to Jerusalem where he knows he will be put to death. But he still heals people, even though he is probably thinking about what will happen to him in Jerusalem. Healing and helping those who are helpless is one of the main deeds that Jesus came to perform, and he is not about to stop.

In this story, Jesus heals ten lepers. Leprosy is a word that people in Jesus' time used for skin diseases that were contagious. If you got close to someone with leprosy, you might get it, too. Leprosy was not like getting poison ivy today—you take some medicine to stop the itching and it goes away in a few days. Leprosy didn't go away very easily. Sometimes it never went away.

In the Old Testament, there were laws about keeping away from lepers so that you wouldn't catch the skin disease. If someone had a skin disease, he had to keep his hair uncombed, wear torn clothes, and keep his face covered. Then he had to walk around saying "unclean, unclean" so people knew to keep away from him. (Imagine having to do that every time you have poison ivy!) Lepers also had to live apart from everyone. They couldn't work—no one would hire them or work with them. All they could do was beg for food to stay alive.

That's how these ten lepers were living. When they see Jesus, they shout to him, "Have pity on us!" They are asking Jesus to heal them so they can live normal lives.

Of course Jesus is willing to have pity on them and heal them. But instead of just healing them on the spot, he tells them to go and show themselves to the priests. The Old Testament law says the priests have to examine anyone who claims to be healed from leprosy, to make sure that the disease is completely gone. The lepers believe that Jesus will heal them, and so they head off to see the priests. On the way, all ten lepers are healed.

Nine of the lepers are Jews and they keep on going to see the priests. They are eager to do what the law says. They can't wait to have the priests say they are healed so they can go back to their families and friends.

But one of the lepers comes back. He throws himself at Jesus' feet and thanks him. He is a Samaritan. When we read the story of the good Samaritan, you learned that Jews and Samaritans did not get along. The Jews looked down on the Samaritans and didn't want anything to do with them.

So why does the Samaritan come back? He comes back to thank Jesus. He can't believe that Jesus, who is Jewish, would heal a Samaritan like him. The Samaritan sees that Jesus cares about everyone, no matter who they are or where they are from. He has learned that Jesus brings healing and kindness to people like him, people on the outside. That is why the Samaritan comes back to thank Jesus and to give praise to God.

People on the outside—like lepers—were more likely to recognize Jesus than those who were not suffering. And Jesus does not push them aside or ignore them. Even as Jesus is walking to Jerusalem to die, he stops and heals them.

<table>
<tr><td>

Lesson

10

</td><td>

Matthew 9:18–26
Jesus Actually Touches
a Dead Girl and a Sick Woman

</td></tr>
</table>

What the Parent Should Know: This story is found in Mark 5:22–43 and Luke 8:41–56 as well. Matthew's version is the shortest and so leaves out some details of the story that are familiar to many (such as: the girl's father's name is Jairus, and Jesus declares, "Little girl, I say to you, get up"). But the heart of the story remains the same in all three versions. In the Old Testament there were many "purity laws" (about what to eat or what to come into contact with) that ensured that the Israelites were a pure people before God, not like the other nations. But the kingdom of God Jesus preaches transcends these purity laws. This story illustrates this principle.

The two healings Jesus performs in this passage must be understood in the context of those Old Testament purity laws (see especially Leviticus 11–15). First, a ruler (of a synagogue, according to Mark and Luke) asks Jesus to come and lay his <u>hand</u> on his <u>dead</u> daughter. According to Numbers 19:11–13, touching a corpse rendered that person unclean, which meant being isolated from the community and barred from worship in the tabernacle. To be reinstated (purified, made clean), the offender had to go through a seven-day period of ritual purification. Failure to do so meant "that person must be cut off from Israel" (Numbers 19:13), meaning banishment from the community (or even execution in some cases, see Leviticus 20:1–5). So, taking the dead girl by the hand was not a casual act but a clear comment on the purity laws: they are no longer binding.

Second, a woman who had been hemorrhaging for twelve years <u>touches</u> Jesus' cloak for healing. According to Leviticus 15:19–33, contact of any sort with a woman during menstruation also made one ritualistically unclean. (In the children's lesson we refer to her as a "very sick woman.") This woman's medical condition also had debilitating social ramifications. Her condition would have kept her from getting married since her husband would not have been allowed to have intercourse with her (Leviticus 18:19). With no husband or children, such a woman would be socially isolated and have no means of financial support. So, this woman is desperate, willing even to encounter a large crowd of people, risking that others contract the impurity, in order to see Jesus and touch his cloak so she can be healed.

In both cases, Jesus turns the tables on Old Testament purity laws. Rather than a corpse or bleeding woman making him unclean, his touch takes their impurity away. He does not contract their impurity; they "contract" his healing power.

Touching a dead corpse and an unclean woman are not random flexing of Jesus' muscles. They "act out" what he teaches elsewhere. In the verses that immediately precede this miracle story, Jesus teaches that the "new wine" of the Gospel cannot be contained in the "old wineskin" of Jewish law (vv. 15–17). These miracles are marks of Jesus' compassion, to be sure. But they are more. They show that the old purity laws, so important to Old Testament Israel, are no longer binding. The gospel that Jesus preaches is not about protecting one's purity but transforming the heart and healing a broken world.

Begin by reading aloud:

> While he was saying this, a ruler came and knelt before him and said, "My daughter has just died. But come and put your hand on her, and she will live." Jesus got up and went with him, and so did his disciples.
>
> Just then a woman who had been subject to bleeding for twelve years came up behind him and touched the edge of his cloak. She said to herself, "If I only touch his cloak, I will be healed."
>
> Jesus turned and saw her. "Take heart, daughter," he said, "your faith has healed you." And the woman was healed from that moment.
>
> When Jesus entered the ruler's house and saw the flute players and the noisy crowd, he said, "Go away. The girl is not dead but asleep." But they laughed at him. After the crowd had been put outside, he went in and took the girl by the hand, and she got up. News of this spread through all that region.

As this story begins, Jesus is in the middle of a conversation with his disciples. He is still talking when a man comes to ask him for help—his daughter has just died and he asks Jesus to touch her so she can live again. As he goes to help the man, Jesus heals a woman who has been sick for a very long time—twelve years. He heals her by *touching* her. And then Jesus helps the man by raising his daughter from the dead. Jesus does this by *touching* her, too.

Sometimes Jesus heals people just by saying so, but here he heals by touching them. In Jesus' day, touching a dead body or a very sick woman was a big problem because the laws in the Old Testament made it very clear that you were not allowed to do either of these things. A dead body or a sick woman like this was "unclean." Whoever touched either one became "unclean" too. That meant that they could not be around other Israelites or worship God in the temple.

The only way "unclean" people could be made "clean" was if a priest sprinkled special cleansing water on them. There is nothing magical about the water itself, but sprinkling was a way of showing that it was OK for the person to be with other Israelites again. But even then the person who had been cleansed would still have to wait another week until he was officially clean. And if the priest did not make him clean, he would be banished—that means he would no longer have any contact with other Israelites and could not worship God anymore in the temple. This would be like being forced to leave your house and your neighborhood by yourself and finding another place to live. Being unclean was a big deal!

So why in the world does Jesus touch this sick woman and this dead girl? Isn't Jesus afraid of becoming unclean? No, he isn't. Jesus touches the woman and the girl, but this does not make Jesus unclean. Instead, by his power, Jesus heals them.

Healing the sick woman and raising a dead girl back to life do more than show how powerful Jesus is. By touching them he shows everyone that the old laws about being clean and unclean are not what is truly important to God. Jesus shows us that God cares more for us and our struggles.

Unit 3

Teachings of Jesus

Jesus' teachings were mainly about the kingdom of heaven, also referred to as the kingdom of God. This kingdom was not far off in the future, nor was Jesus typically referring to the afterlife. This kingdom is here and now. Jesus is the king who has come to set up a kingdom made up of people who follow Jesus' teachings—who live their lives loving God and loving others more than themselves. The lessons below examine the character of those who are part of this kingdom (Lessons 11 and 12) as well as the character of King Jesus (Lessons 13–15).

<table>
<tr><td>

Lesson

11

</td><td align="right">

Luke 14:7–14

God Loves the Rich and the Poor the Same

</td></tr>
</table>

What the Parent Should Know: The context for this passage begins in v. 1 with dinner at a Pharisee's house. It is not unusual for Jesus to associate with Pharisees, since, theologically, he is one himself. Pharisees represented the mainstream of Jewish teaching at the time, and belief in the resurrection of the dead was one of several beliefs that distinguished them from the Sadducees (see Luke 20:17–40). Another distinctive mark of the Sadducees was recognizing only the Torah (Pentateuch) as authoritative for Jewish belief. Pharisees treated all of the Bible as authoritative.

In this lesson we join the dinner conversation at v. 7. Jesus tells his exalted dinner guests that they should humble themselves and exalt those in humble circumstances. In the kingdom of heaven, social convention is turned on its head. There is no room for self-promotion, including for those who hold legitimate positions of spiritual authority, such as the dinner host and guests in this passage.

The Pharisee who is hosting the dinner is socially prominent, and Jesus notices that the guests are scrambling for the seats of honor near the head (vv. 7–11). People of prominence were usually given seats at the head of the table; for them to sit lower down would have been socially awkward. Jesus does not deny that important people are given seats in places befitting their status (vv. 8–9). Instead, he is talking more generally about self-importance. Jesus says to his followers, "Rather than jockeying for position to promote your own status, humble yourself. If in the end you are honored because of your position of authority, fine, but let it be by others."

We can imagine how socially awkward—even offensive—it must have been for the guests to hear Jesus draw attention to their behavior. But even at a dinner party, Jesus is more concerned about preaching the kingdom of heaven than rubbing elbows with the rich and famous.

In vv. 12–14 Jesus continues on the theme of humility but from a different angle. His focus here is not on the guests taking the best seats, but rather on whom the host chooses to invite. From the point of view of social convention, Jesus' host would naturally invite to dinner those of like status, those who make him look good and would return the invitation—in other words, he would naturally invite people for his own benefit.

But here, too, the kingdom of heaven operates by different rules. "How do I maintain status?" is not a legitimate question in the kingdom of heaven. Rather, Jesus tells the host to invite those of humble circumstances for their benefit: the poor and infirm, those who can give nothing back. Invite such as these and you will be repaid at the "resurrection of the righteous" (v. 14; meaning followers of Jesus will be judged by their actions and rewarded accordingly, e.g., 2 Corinthians 5:10).

Jesus tells the guests at a dinner party that they should think nothing of the status they have legitimately earned. Jesus tells the host that he should go out of the way to associate with those who are at the polar opposite rung on the social ladder. Both of these messages were wholly countercultural, as they are now, but it is what the kingdom requires. The exalted, on equal footing with everyone else, are servants of the king.

When he noticed how the guests picked the places of honor at the table, he told them this parable: "When someone invites you to a wedding feast, do not take the place of honor, for a person more distinguished than you may have been invited. If so, the host who invited both of you will come and say to you, 'Give this man your seat.' Then, humiliated, you will have to take the least important place. But when you are invited, take the lowest place, so that when your host comes, he will say to you, 'Friend, move up to a better place.' Then you will be honored in the presence of all your fellow guests. For everyone who exalts himself will be humbled, and he who humbles himself will be exalted."

Then Jesus said to his host, "When you give a luncheon or dinner, do not invite your friends, your brothers or relatives, or your rich neighbors; if you do, they may invite you back and so you will be repaid. But when you give a banquet, invite the poor, the crippled, the lame, the blind, and you will be blessed. Although they cannot repay you, you will be repaid at the resurrection of the righteous."

Jesus is having dinner at the house of an important Pharisee. Pharisees were powerful and respected religious leaders who taught people about God. When it comes time to eat, the guests all try to take the best seats at the table. When Jesus sees this, he decides to teach them a lesson. In God's eyes, the rich and the poor are the same.

In Jesus' day, the best seats were the ones closest to the host—the person giving the dinner. The host was supposed to seat the most important people at the dinner close to him—and the less important people further away. So at this dinner, everyone wants to get the best seats at the table. This will show everyone else just how powerful they are.

Imagine that you are at a birthday party. When it is time to sit down and open presents and eat cake, the birthday girl sits at the head of the table. Everyone wants to sit as close to the birthday girl as possible. If they sit too far away they feel left out. Maybe some of the kids are trying to grab the best seats before anyone else.

Jesus tells the dinner guests that God does not want them to take the best seats. Even though they really are respected (because they are leaders among the Jews), Jesus says they should be humble and take the worst seats and leave the best seats for others. This is what Jesus is teaching the guests: In Jesus' kingdom, there is no place for anyone—even leaders—to act more important than others. Leaders serve God just like everyone else.

Jesus has something to say to the host, too. The host invited all the powerful and important people to his party. He thinks this will make him look even more important to everyone else. He also thinks that if he invites them, they will all invite him to their houses for dinner.

Imagine another birthday party. This time, instead of inviting his best friends, the birthday boy invites people who have no friends—people who are lonely or new to the neighborhood and don't have many chances to go to fun birthday parties. Imagine a party like that, where the host thinks more about the guests than he thinks about getting presents or being the center of attention.

This is what Jesus is telling the host: Even though you are powerful and respected, don't just invite people who will make you look good. Invite the weak and lonely and show them that God loves them just as much.

Jesus has a different message for the guests and for the host, but Jesus is still teaching them the same big lesson. Jesus tells them all that, in Jesus' kingdom, leaders are not more important to God than others just because they are leaders. There is no place in the kingdom of heaven for that kind of thinking.

<table>
<tr><td>Lesson

12</td><td></td></tr>
</table>

Luke 7:36–50
No One's Sins are too Big for God to Forgive

What the Parent Should Know: While Jesus is at the home of Simon the Pharisee for dinner, we meet a "woman who lived a sinful life" (v. 37). It is possible she is a prostitute, but there is no clear indication of what she did to earn this reputation (she could also be an adulteress, for example). The woman comes over to Jesus, wets his feet with her tears, wipes them with her hair, kisses his feet, and pours perfume on them. Rather than recoil at the scene, Jesus lets it play out. The woman has sinned much, but Jesus shows her the love of God and forgives her when the teachers of Israel only shun her. Having seen the love of God in action, the woman "loves much" (v. 47) in return.

We see here, as we see so often in the Gospels, Jesus' willingness to be associated with "sinners," i.e., those who fall far short of obeying Israel's law and are ostracized for it. (And if this story sounds familiar, it is very similar to the story of Jesus being anointed for his burial, Year One, Lesson 36.) Sinful women—whether prostitutes or adulteresses—were considered among the worst types of sinners in Jesus' day, in part because the Old Testament looks down upon both with disdain (Leviticus 20:20 and 19:29).

In our culture it is common to be repulsed when "undesirables" invade our personal space, let alone cry on our shoulders and hang on us. We would likely pull back from such an awkward situation and move away to reclaim our space. But this sinful woman is all over Jesus, and rather than shrinking back in embarrassment and offense, he just keeps quiet. The reason for Jesus' actions is made clear in the story he tells beginning in v. 41. Like the debtor in that story, the woman's great sin is not an impediment to forgiveness, as the Pharisee seems to think in v. 39. Rather, her great sin is the reason why, when forgiven, she will love God greatly. Her present sin is not Jesus' focus. Instead, Jesus looks ahead to what she will be once the sin is forgiven.

Simon thinks Jesus is mishandling a clear black-and-white situation: such a woman is to be detested, or at least shunned. He is repulsed that a woman like this would touch Jesus—and even more repulsed that Jesus would let her. After all, if Jesus really were a prophet, he would know who this woman was and act accordingly. But, as usual, Jesus turns the tables. He is a prophet, and precisely for that reason he brings forgiveness to this woman. The Pharisee host seems determined to keep God's grace as far away from her as possible. Jesus, however, turns the woman's scandalous act of love into an object lesson for Israel's leaders: this is what the deep love of God looks like (vv. 44–47).

Simon and his guests are repulsed, but they are being given a crash course in the kingdom of God. Through his response to this woman, Jesus shows what kind of people make up his kingdom: forgiven sinners, embraced by God's love, whose hearts are healed and who love much in return.

Begin by reading aloud:

> Now one of the Pharisees invited Jesus to have dinner with him, so he went to the Pharisee's house and reclined at the table. When a woman who had lived a sinful life in that town learned that Jesus was eating at the Pharisee's house, she brought an alabaster jar of perfume, and as she stood behind him at his feet weeping, she began to wet his feet

with her tears. Then she wiped them with her hair, kissed them, and poured perfume on them.

When the Pharisee who had invited him saw this, he said to himself, "If this man were a prophet, he would know who is touching him and what kind of woman she is—that she is a sinner."

Jesus answered him, "Simon, I have something to tell you."

"Tell me, teacher," he said.

"Two men owed money to a certain moneylender. One owed him five hundred denarii, and the other fifty. Neither of them had the money to pay him back, so he canceled the debts of both. Now which of them will love him more?"

Simon replied, "I suppose the one who had the bigger debt canceled."

"You have judged correctly," Jesus said.

Then he turned toward the woman and said to Simon, "Do you see this woman? I came into your house. You did not give me any water for my feet, but she wet my feet with her tears and wiped them with her hair. You did not give me a kiss, but this woman, from the time I entered, has not stopped kissing my feet. You did not put oil on my head, but she has poured perfume on my feet. Therefore, I tell you, her many sins have been forgiven—for she loved much. But he who has been forgiven little loves little."

Then Jesus said to her, "Your sins are forgiven."

The other guests began to say among themselves, "Who is this who even forgives sins?"

Jesus said to the woman, "Your faith has saved you; go in peace."

In this story, Jesus is having dinner at the house of a Pharisee named Simon. The guests are lying down ready for dinner. (In Jesus' day, people ate lying down, facing in toward the food, not on chairs and tables as today.) While they are eating, a woman who has lived a sinful life walks in. "Sinful" means she has broken God's law again and again.

The guests say that a sinful woman like this has no business marching into Simon's house without being invited. But the woman walks over to Jesus and starts touching him. She is crying. Her tears fall on Jesus' feet, and she wipes them off with her hair. Then she puts perfume all over Jesus' feet. The Pharisees are shocked and embarrassed.

Imagine you are sitting at the dinner table with your family and some guests from church. Suddenly, in bursts a relative you have not seen for a long time. He has been in jail for stealing. "What is he doing here?!" Then

    Lesson 12: No One's Sins are too Big for God to Forgive

he walks over to your father and begins crying all over him and hanging on him. The relative had stolen a lot of money from your father, but now he wants to be forgiven because he is truly sorry. How would that make you feel? Would you believe him? Would you want him to stay or leave?

Well, when this woman barges into Simon's dinner party, Simon wants her to get out right away. He thinks this woman is too sinful to be around. He says, "If Jesus is really a prophet, he will know what kind of a woman this is and he will keep away from her. So why does Jesus just sit there and do nothing?"

Jesus knows the woman is a great sinner, but he does not try to get away from her. Instead, he wants to forgive her. The woman is crying and wiping his feet because she knows Jesus will forgive her. She is crying because she is happy: even her great sins aren't too much for Jesus to forgive.

Jesus shows that his kingdom is made up of people like this woman: people who are forgiven for the wrong they have done because God loves them. Simon and his guests do not yet understand that no one is too sinful for God's forgiveness. And someone whose sin is so great will love God greatly when they are forgiven, just as Jesus says.

<table>
<tr><td>Lesson
13</td><td>John 10:11–21
Jesus is the Shepherd
who Loves His Sheep</td></tr>
</table>

What the Parent Should Know: This passage is one of seven "I AM" passages in the Gospel of John (the others are 6:35; 8:12; 10:9; 11:25; 14:6; 15:1, 5). In these seven passages, Jesus makes claims about who he is, always using the same wording: "I am. . ." All of the "I AM" passages are metaphors: I AM the gate (v. 10:9), light of the world (8:12), vine (15:1), etc. In this passage Jesus is the good shepherd—he is guiding his sheep into the presence of his loving Father.

The phrase "I AM" clearly echoes Exodus 3:14. When God was about to deliver the Israelites from Egypt, he announced his name to Moses as "I AM." Further, by saying he is the good shepherd, Jesus is alluding to God's role in shepherding the Israelites out of Egypt (e.g., Psalms 77:20 and 100:3). By saying "I AM the good shepherd," Jesus is claiming that God is present in him to deliver his people once again. In other words, Jesus is claiming divine status.

The implications of Jesus' words were not lost on his audience. No serious Jew could claim to be the "I AM" walking among them. Many of the people who heard Jesus talk like this thought he was "demon-possessed and raving mad" (v. 20). Yet, the fact that Jesus had healed the blind (v. 21) gives some of the people pause: Can crazy people heal the blind? Perhaps there is something to Jesus' claim.

If Jesus is the good shepherd, that makes his followers the sheep. But unlike the Old Testament where "sheep" refers to Israel, Jesus' followers include "other sheep" (v. 16), in other words Gentiles as well as Jews. Including outsiders among his people is a key theme in John and the other Gospels.

As the good shepherd, Jesus is not a distant leader of some diverse group of people who happen to like what he says. He is not a commander barking orders or a king handing down edicts. He is a gentle guide for his people, giving them great care and attention. In fact, the good shepherd goes above and beyond the call of normal shepherd duty. Unlike a mere hired hand who runs at the first sign of danger (v. 12), Jesus is fiercely protective of his sheep; he is even willing to die for them (vv. 11, 15). Shepherds would normally do everything within reason to protect the sheep, but to die for their safety— well—they're only sheep, after all. But the good shepherd loves his sheep and will not abandon them to danger.

What is most startling of all about this good shepherd is the intimacy between Jesus and his sheep, which echoes the intimacy between Jesus and the Father (v. 14). Jesus' followers are bound in love to Jesus and to the Father, which is a prominent theme in John's Gospel (e.g., 17:20–23). The picture Jesus draws here is startling and a deep mystery of the Christian faith, but the best word to describe this intimacy is love. Jesus, the good shepherd, loves his sheep with the same love that exists between him and the Father.

The implications of this "I AM" claim are clear: Jesus is a loving shepherd of God's people who leads his sheep into the presence of a loving Father.

Begin by reading aloud:

I am the good shepherd. The good shepherd lays down his life for the sheep. The hired hand is not the shepherd who owns the sheep. So when he sees the wolf coming, he abandons the sheep and runs away. Then the wolf attacks the flock and scatters it. The man runs away because he is a hired hand and cares nothing for the sheep.

I am the good shepherd; I know my sheep and my sheep know me—just as the Father knows me and I know the Father—and I lay down my life for the sheep. I have other sheep that are not of this sheep pen. I must bring them also. They too will listen to my voice, and there shall be one flock and one shepherd. The reason my Father loves me is that I lay down my life—only to take it up again. No one takes it from me, but I lay it down of my own accord. I have authority to lay it down and authority to take it up again. This command I received from my Father."

At these words the Jews were again divided. Many of them said, "He is demon-possessed and raving mad. Why listen to him?"

But others said, "These are not the sayings of a man possessed by a demon. Can a demon open the eyes of the blind?"

In this story, Jesus says, "I am the good shepherd." Jesus means that those who follow him are like sheep and Jesus the shepherd will show them how much God loves them. In fact, Jesus says that he loves his sheep the same way Jesus and his heavenly Father love each other. Nothing can keep Jesus and his Father from loving each other. So that means that nothing can keep Jesus from loving and caring for us, his sheep.

Jesus says that he loves his sheep so much, he would even die for them. A normal shepherd would not do this. He lets his sheep graze and then brings them back safely into their pen. He protects his sheep as best as he can, but if he sees a ferocious wolf coming, he won't get in the way. He will let the wolf grab a sheep and leave. But Jesus says he is a different kind of shepherd. He is a good shepherd.

Some of the people who hear Jesus talking like this think he is crazy. They know that in the Old Testament, God is called Israel's shepherd. When Jesus says, "I am the good shepherd," it sounds like he is saying that he is God. Jesus also says that he knows the Father and the Father knows him. Jesus is saying that he is closer to God than anyone else. Some of those listening think that only a crazy person would talk like this.

But the listeners are wrong; Jesus is not crazy. He is the good shepherd, but not everyone listening understands. He will always care for his sheep, the people who follow him. Nothing will ever stop Jesus, because he loves his sheep the same way Jesus and his Father love each other. That love never ends.

Jesus is Greater than Death

What the Parent Should Know: The fifth of John's "I AM" statements (see Lesson 13) is "I AM the resurrection and the life." Like the other "I AM" statements, this one describes who Jesus is, not what he can do. So, in 6:35, Jesus is the bread of life, not someone who gives bread; in 8:12, he is the light of the world, not one who gives light. So, by claiming to be resurrection and life, Jesus means that he is the end to death itself. He will show this later in his own resurrection. Traveling back to Judea from Bethany (11:7) to raise his friend Lazarus is a preview.

Judea was a place of "double-death" for Jesus. First, Lazarus was already dead for four days (v. 17), a fact that Martha laments greatly (v. 21). Second, Judea meant certain death for Jesus. Earlier the Jews had tried to stone Jesus (10:31), but he escaped (10:39). To go back to Judea is virtual suicide, and Thomas even resigns himself to the fact (11:16; Thomas's words are borne out in vv. 45–57: no sooner does Jesus raise Lazarus than the chief priests and Pharisees plot to kill Jesus, which introduces the Passion Week in chapter 12). So, why would Jesus go to such a hopeless place? Jesus' willingness to return to Judea is not a heroic show of bravery or even a demonstration of his love for his friend. Rather, Judea is the ideal location for Jesus to show "I AM the resurrection and the life": for Lazarus, for Jesus himself, and for all who believe in him.

When he arrives, Jesus assures Martha that her brother will rise again (v. 23). Martha assumes Jesus is talking about the resurrection that will happen "at the last day" (v. 24), meaning at the end of the world (see Daniel 12:1–4). But Jesus means now, not later. Jesus is not denying the idea of a future resurrection. He means that his very presence among them means the future has invaded the present. Resurrection is no longer something that merely will happen—it has already begun. Death not only will be conquered. Its end has already arrived in the person of Jesus. That is what Jesus means by saying, "I AM the resurrection and the life." Wherever he is, death does not have the final say.

The conquering of death is a spiritual truth in addition to a physical truth: resurrection and life already now touch all those who live in Jesus and believe in him (v. 26). All who believe have already "crossed over from death to life," as Jesus says in John 5:24. But now with the raising of Lazarus, Jesus begins to show that the death he conquers is physical as well.

The raising of Lazarus is not a rescue story where Jesus comes sweeping in to snatch someone from death. The story is about Jesus—not what he can do, but who he is.

Begin by reading aloud:

Lazarus is the brother of Mary and Martha and a close friend of Jesus. Jesus hears that Lazarus is very sick and about to die, so he travels to Judea where Lazarus is. Judea is dangerous for Jesus. Some of the people in Judea are angry with him. Jesus was there once before and told the people that they could only know God by listening to him. Some of those listening wanted to stone Jesus to death, but Jesus escaped. Now Jesus goes back to Judea because of Lazarus. Here is what happened.

> On his arrival, Jesus found that Lazarus had already been in the tomb for four days. Bethany was less than two miles from Jerusalem, and many Jews had come to Martha and Mary to comfort them in the loss of their brother. When Martha heard that Jesus was coming, she went out to meet him, but Mary stayed at home.
>
> "Lord," Martha said to Jesus, "if you had been here, my brother would not have died. But I know that even now God will give you whatever you ask."
>
> Jesus said to her, "Your brother will rise again."
>
> Martha answered, "I know he will rise again in the resurrection at the last day."
>
> Jesus said to her, "I am the resurrection and the life. He who believes in me will live, even though he dies; and whoever lives and believes in me will never die. Do you believe this?"
>
> "Yes, Lord," she told him, "I believe that you are the Christ, the Son of God, who was to come into the world."

By the time Jesus gets to Lazarus' house, the house is full of people comforting Mary and Martha. Lazarus died four days ago. Now Lazarus is in a tomb, which is a small cave with a big rock in front of the opening.

Martha is brokenhearted. She comes up to Jesus and says, "If only you had gotten here sooner, you could have healed Lazarus. But now he is dead and it is too late."

Jesus tells Martha that Lazarus will not stay dead but will rise again. Martha thinks that means way in the future, at the end of the world. But Jesus is not talking about God raising Lazarus from the dead one day in the future. Jesus means he is going to raise Lazarus right now. That is what Jesus means when he says to Martha "I am the resurrection and the life."

Death does not have any power over Jesus. So he is not afraid to march right into Judea, even though he knows people there want to arrest him and have him put to death. Death does not have any power over Lazarus, either, because Jesus is there to raise him from the dead. Jesus tells Martha that he is going to raise Lazarus from the dead, and a little later in the story that is what he does.

Jesus also tells Martha that death has no power over anybody who believes in him. That doesn't mean that if you believe in Jesus you won't die. Everyone dies. But throughout your whole life, no matter where you are or what you do, you belong to Jesus. Even when you die for real, you still belong to Jesus, and he will one day raise from the dead all who believe in him. Raising Lazarus from the dead shows everyone that Jesus can do that.

<table>
<tr><td>Lesson
15</td><td style="text-align:right">John 15:1–8

Staying Connected to Jesus</td></tr>
</table>

What the Parent Should Know: In this passage we see the last of the seven I AM statements in John's Gospel (see Lesson 13). Jesus is speaking to his disciples and says he is the vine and they are the branches. This means that the disciples—and all believers after them—can only "bear fruit" by "remaining" in Jesus. This passage teaches that Jesus' followers must remain "connected" to him as they live out their mission of living and spreading the gospel.

A glimpse at the Old Testament will help explain this metaphor. In the Old Testament, God is the gardener who cares for Israel, his vines (see Isaiah 5:1–7). The vines are to bear fruit, which means living in faithfulness to the covenant (the Law). Israel's faithfulness will spread news of Israel's God by attracting the nations to him.

But in the end, Israel did not bear such fruit. Instead of attracting the nations to God, Israel was taken into exile in Babylon. By saying "I AM the vine," Jesus claims to be taking over Israel's role. Jesus is the true vine, the true Israel, who will fulfill Israel's mission of faithfulness to God and reconciliation of the nations.

Jesus is the true vine and he extends the metaphor to include his followers: they are the branches that grow from the vine, and _they_ are to bear fruit. Jesus and his followers _together_ are the "new Israel"(see Galatians 6:16), the true fruit-bearing vine. Understanding the church as the "new Israel" is also a pivotal point made throughout the New Testament. Jesus calls to himself a people made up of Jew and Gentile to continue Israel's mission. The church is the new Israel that continues the mission begun by Jesus in his teachings, death, and resurrection—the reconciling of the nations to the true God.

Therefore, the metaphor of the vine and branches is not a catchy way of saying "you need Jesus." It gets at the heart of New Testament teaching: a new people (branch) "grows out" of the crucified and risen Lord (vine). As a branch, this new people of God has its source of life in the vine. Individuals can only bear fruit by staying connected to the vine, by "remaining" in Jesus (vv. 4–5). "Remaining" means more than believing things about Jesus. It means a continual attitude of trust and surrender to Jesus—in other words, more than "believing" intellectually a set of doctrines.

In v. 6, failure to remain in Jesus means the branches will wither and be burned. Along with vine, branches, and fruit, fire is a metaphor that conveys a deep truth: apart from Jesus, a disciple is as useless as a withered branch, fit for nothing but being burned up.

The metaphor of "vine and branches" illustrates the absolutely vital, life-giving, non-negotiable connection Christians have to Jesus as they fulfill God's mission to reconcile the world. The mission is a daunting task to be sure, but not if the branch remains in the vine.

Begin by reading aloud:

> I am the true vine, and my Father is the gardener. He cuts off every branch in me that bears no fruit, while every branch that does bear fruit he prunes so that it will be even more fruitful. You are already clean because of the word I have spoken to you. Remain in me, and I will remain in you. No branch can bear fruit by itself; it must remain in the vine. Neither can you bear fruit unless you remain in me.
>
> I am the vine; you are the branches. If a man remains in me and I in him, he will bear much fruit; apart from me you can do nothing. If anyone does not remain in me, he is like a branch that is thrown away and withers; such branches are picked up, thrown into the fire, and burned. If you remain in me and my words remain in you, ask whatever

you wish, and it will be given you. This is to my Father's glory, that
you bear much fruit, showing yourselves to be my disciples.

Jesus is talking to his disciples. He knows he is going to be crucified soon. So he is telling the disciples to remember what he taught them and to keep following him always. That way they will be ready to keep teaching others about God.

Jesus explains what he means in a way that will help the disciples remember. Jesus says, "Think of me as a vine. You are branches that grow from the vine. If you don't continue to grow, you will dry up and break off. Branches like that aren't good for anything other than being tossed into a fire."

Jesus is talking about grape vines here, which were very common back then. Most of us don't see grape vines very often, so think of a shade tree instead.

Where I live there are a lot of shade trees. One of them is huge, probably 150 feet high with a trunk a grown-up can't even get his arms halfway around. This tree is also completely dead. In the spring, when all the other trees are budding, this tree just sits there—as dry and lifeless as it was in the winter. This tree has stopped producing leaves—like the vines in Jesus' story that have stopped bearing grapes.

A tree like that has to be cut down. It is useless. It doesn't give off any shade for us, nor does it grow leaves and acorns for food for animals. It is also dangerous. The branches—some of them very big—are so dry that they come crashing down during a strong wind.

When those dead branches fall down, I pick them up and put them in a woodpile in the backyard. In the winter we burn that wood in our fireplace. And that's what I need to do with the whole tree. I need to get someone to cut it down and chop it up so I can use it for firewood.

Why does Jesus tell a story about vines, branches, and fruit? Jesus is telling his disciples that if they forget what he taught them and stop trusting him, they will become like dried-up branches with no fruit growing on them. Disciples like that will not be ready to obey God or teach others about God. But those who keep following Jesus are like green branches with a lot of fruit. They will love God and show others that God loves them, too.

The Sermon on the Mount

In the Sermon on the Mount, we must keep in mind that Jesus is teaching the people what it means to be citizens of the kingdom of heaven (or of God). This kingdom is a topic of Jesus' teaching throughout the Gospels, but especially in the Sermon on the Mount. When we hear "kingdom of *heaven*" today, we may be inclined to think of a kingdom that is not part of this world—either a kingdom "up there" somewhere or a kingdom we will one day see after we die. This can lead to a misreading of the Sermon on the Mount as a list of things one has to do in order to earn salvation and make it to heaven.

The kingdom Jesus is talking about, however, is the kingdom he is building right then and there. This is not a kingdom *in* heaven, but a kingdom *from* heaven, a kingdom *from* God. In other words "kingdom of heaven" does not tell us about the kingdom's location, but of its origin and therefore of its character. This idea is summarized well in one line of the Lord's Prayer: "Your will be done *on earth as it is in heaven.*" King Jesus was sent by the Father to establish this kingdom, proclaiming to people the Good News that the kingdom has come to them.

Jesus in his preaching is showing the people more clearly the character of God, the character that should be embodied by citizens of the kingdom right now. These characteristics of the citizens of the kingdom are typically the very opposite of what the religious leaders of the time were teaching. Also, Jesus' teachings often go beyond what the Old Testament itself prescribes. This kingdom is "new wine" that cannot be contained in "old wineskins" (Matthew 9:17). The kingdom of heaven is ready to burst forth and expose the hypocrisy of the religious leaders as well as the incompleteness of Israel's own story in the Old Testament. All followers of Jesus are to be taught these new ways, not to earn God's favor but to enjoy his blessings.

<table>
<tr><td>**Lesson 16**</td><td align="right">**Matthew 6:1–4**
Give to the Needy
without Showing Off</td></tr>
</table>

What the Parent Should Know: Giving to the needy is a command that goes back to the Old Testament. In a male-dominated society, "needy" included widows and orphans who were economically disadvantaged in the absence of a husband or father (e.g., Exodus 22:22–24). Aliens—non-Israelites in Israelite territory—were also among the needy, because foreigners were often subject to mistreatment in the ancient world (as they are today). Israelites, however, were commanded to care for them, because they, too, had been aliens in Egypt (Exodus 22:21).

In this passage, Jesus assumes his listeners are fully aware of this command. But Jesus is doing more than simply reminding them. He is challenging them to see that the kingdom of heaven is not about outward obedience but inner transformation, where no one sees except for God himself. Giving to the needy is not to be a way of building up one's ego or status before others. It is a way of letting go of such self-centered behaviors and communing with God instead. Giving to the needy is a spiritual exercise for the giver.

We learn here that giving to the needy is an "act of righteousness" (v. 1). The other acts of righteousness in this chapter are prayer (vv. 5–14) and fasting (vv. 16–18). These acts are expected of members of the kingdom of heaven and are the basis of God's future rewards (vv. 1 and 4). Although Jesus does not explain exactly what he means by "reward," other New Testament teachings make clear that while salvation is by God's grace, God will still judge according to one's works (1 Corinthians 3:12–15). These acts are not the basis of salvation, but reflect what saved people are to act like.

For those who are members of the kingdom, giving to the needy is an act of devotion to God, not to oneself. Those who draw attention to themselves are called "hypocrites" (v. 2), which means they are just "acting" the part, pretending (which is what the word means in Greek).

> Be careful not to do your "acts of righteousness" before men, to be seen by them. If you do, you will have no reward from your Father in heaven.
>
> So when you give to the needy, do not announce it with trumpets, as the hypocrites do in the synagogues and on the streets, to be honored by men. I tell you the truth, they have received their reward in full. But when you give to the needy, do not let your left hand know what your right hand is doing, so that your giving may be in secret. Then your Father, who sees what is done in secret, will reward you.

In this story, Jesus tells his listeners to make sure they give to the needy. Helping those who cannot help themselves is commanded by law in the Old Testament. Jesus also tells them that when they give to the needy, they should not show off about it. Jesus says it is wrong to give so that others will notice. Instead, Jesus says that they should give without anyone knowing about it except God.

In Jesus' days, the streets were filled with people who could not help themselves. Women could not work like they do today, so they relied on their husbands for food and shelter. If the husband died and left the woman a widow, she had to rely on the kindness of others to live. The same goes for orphans. Without a father and mother to take care of them, they relied on the kindness of others to get by. Jesus calls giving to the needy an act of righteousness, which means that giving to the needy is the right thing to do in God's eyes.

It feels good when we help those in need. Maybe you are on an outing and someone has forgotten his money. You buy him an ice cream and an adult says, "That is SO KIND of you!" We feel good when people notice when we do something like that.

There is nothing wrong with being noticed like this. Sometimes those who are around us just happen to notice that we are being kind. But what if we are kind only because an adult is watching? We help someone just to be noticed. Jesus is saying this is wrong because, when we help someone in need, we are actually serving God. We can't serve God when we are thinking about making ourselves look good.

Jesus says not to make a big deal of it when we do something kind for the needy. When someone makes a big deal out of it, Jesus says that is like blowing a trumpet every time you do a good deed. That is pretty funny if you stop to think about it. Imagine actually walking around the house and blowing a trumpet to let everyone know every time you were kind to someone!

Jesus talks a lot about being kind to others and helping those who need our help. But Jesus reminds us that we are really serving God when we do those things, not trying to draw attention to ourselves. No one else needs to notice when we are kind. God notices, and that's what counts.

<table>
<tr><td>Lesson
17</td><td>Matthew 6:19–24
You Cannot Serve God
and Another</td></tr>
</table>

What the Parent Should Know: This passage is about two treasures, two eyes, and two masters. All three illustrations support each other and make the same general point, which is summarized at the end of v. 24: you cannot serve God and anything else. You will inevitably serve one or the other, not both.

Jesus begins by talking about two treasures, one earthly and the other heavenly. Since Jesus mentions money in v. 24, "earthly treasure" should be understood literally: money, things, possessions. This is not a trivial point. Which of us does not spend his or her time amassing possessions? But earthly treasure is not something worth storing up because it does not last. It will either diminish naturally in time (by "moth and rust") or will be taken by thieves. Earthly treasure by definition is something that <u>will</u> come to naught, which is why earthly treasure is not where one's "heart" should be. "Heart" is not just the seat of the emotions, as it is normally understood today. In the Bible "heart" is more comprehensive, involving the emotions, the will, and the mind. It is another way of saying "the whole person." Where your treasure is, there <u>you</u> are. You are defined by what you store up.

Hence, the true disciple stores up heavenly treasure. That does not mean walking around with one's thoughts on heaven "up there" somewhere, never giving a thought to clothing, health insurance, grocery shopping, or saving up for a vacation. The context of this passage will help us here. Judging by the eighteen verses that precede this passage (see Lesson 16), "treasures in heaven" refers to the "acts of righteousness": caring for the needy, prayer, and fasting. These are the things we are to "store up," like storing up canned goods and other provisions when you know a massive storm is coming. Being a disciple means being very intentional in doing those activities with which God is pleased. Whatever we are intentional about—wherever our "heart" is—that is where we will find our stored-up treasure.

The two eyes illustrate the same principle. It was thought back then that the eye was actually a source of light: it illuminated objects. Jesus works with this idea and turns it inward. A good eye illuminates "the whole body" with light. Like "heart" above, "whole body" means the whole person. "Light" is a metaphor for a life lived in harmony with God. When our intentions—our "eyes"—are focused on pleasing God, our lives are illuminated, in harmony with God. The eye focused on amassing wealth is the "bad eye" (v. 23), which will plunge one's life into darkness, or disharmony with God.

In v. 24, Jesus sums it all up by saying, "You cannot serve two masters": you cannot store two types of treasure, and you cannot simultaneously have a good eye and a bad eye. Jesus is not saying that one <u>should not</u> serve two masters, but that it is <u>impossible</u> to do so. You can only love and be devoted to one master, since the two masters in question—God and money—(mammon in some translations) have opposite interests.

Far from being a peripheral piece of advice, Jesus' words about material possessions are a profound challenge to how many view their daily existence. We cannot escape "things." We actually need them. But, members of the kingdom of heaven do not "store them," do not focus on them, and do not serve them. The disciple's heart—his whole being—belongs elsewhere.

Begin by reading aloud:

Do not store up for yourselves treasures on earth, where moth and rust destroy, and where thieves break in and steal. But store up for yourselves treasures in heaven, where moth and rust do not destroy, and where thieves do not break in and steal. For where your treasure is, there your heart will be also.

The eye is the lamp of the body. If your eyes are good, your whole body will be full of light. But if your eyes are bad, your whole body will be full of darkness. If then the light within you is darkness, how great is that darkness!

No one can serve two masters. Either he will hate the one and
love the other, or he will be devoted to the one and despise the other.
You cannot serve both God and Money.

In this story, Jesus is talking to a large crowd about a choice everyone needs to make—whether to serve God or to think only of what they want. Jesus says that you can't do both, but have to choose. He explains what he means by talking about two treasures—earthly treasures and heavenly treasures.

Earthly treasures are the things we own and the money we have. Jesus says that sooner or later all of these things—money, clothes, cars, toys—will either rot, crumble, break, or be stolen by someone. Heavenly treasures are not things you own but what you do to serve God—like giving to the needy, being kind to people around you, and loving your family. Heavenly treasures like this never get old, rot, or get stolen.

Jesus says you can't build up both treasures at the same time. Imagine that you are collecting a set of matchbox cars or a family of dolls. You only need one more to complete your collection. You love this collection, and you want that last thing more than anything! But if you buy that last thing, you won't be able to help your friend who doesn't have any toys at all. So, you have to choose. Will you complete your collection, or will you help your friend? You can't do both. You have to do one or the other.

Jesus explains what he means another way. He talks about two types of eyes: good eyes and bad eyes. "Good eye" is a way of saying that you live your life wanting to please God. "Bad eye" is another way of saying "earthly treasures." Someone with a bad eye is always looking to see how many more things he can own. For people like that, getting more things is more important than serving God.

Jesus says that everyone who is a part of his kingdom has to make a choice. Will they have a good eye or a bad eye? Will they collect heavenly treasure or earthly treasure? In other words, Jesus is asking the people whether they will put God and others first in their lives or put themselves first. Jesus says you can't choose both. You have to choose one or the other. When we learn to choose to serve God every day, we will grow to love God more and more.

Lesson 18

Be Honest With Yourself Before You Judge Others

What the Parent Should Know: This passage is summed up in the famous saying of verse one: "Do not judge or you will be judged." This does not mean that followers of Jesus should refrain from exercising wisdom and discernment or being critical of others if need be. Rather, Jesus is saying that spiritual discernment of others begins with humble and unflinching self-assessment.

Those who judge others with an unreflective "better-than" spirit can expect the same treatment from others (v. 2). Jesus returns to this same thought in v. 12: "Do to others as you would have them do to you." In other words, in v. 2, Jesus is not talking about some divine tit-for-tat. He is saying that the quality of your life comes back to you, one way or another. If you focus all your attention on the faults of others, you will find that others focus their attention on your faults.

To refuse to take a spiritual inventory of oneself is to be hypocritical (v. 5), which means, as we saw in Lesson 16, to "play a part." A judgmental person only appears to be a follower of Jesus outwardly, whereas a true disciple is marked by honesty and humility about his own spiritual corruption. Jesus' metaphor of the speck of sawdust vs. the plank illustrates the point. Rather than being quick to run other people's lives, a true disciple—a citizen of the kingdom of heaven—is honest, humble, and truthful about his own very obvious shortcomings.

Taking the plank out of one's own eye does more than just foster inner spiritual growth. Taking out your own plank allows you to "see clearly" (v. 5) enough to take the speck out of the eye of the other. Refraining from judgmentalism does not mean there is never a time to see others for what they really are. Rather, you cannot see others as they really are until you see yourself that way first.

This is where v. 6 comes in. Although we will not deal with this in the student lesson, it fills out the thought:

Do not give dogs what is sacred; do not throw your pearls to pigs. If you do, they may trample them under their feet, and then turn and tear you to pieces.

Left alone this verse is puzzling, but taken with vv. 1–5 it makes sense. Dogs were not pets but scavengers and were looked upon with contempt (15:26–27). Pigs were unclean for Jews and were treated with disgust (8:32; see Leviticus 11:7). Jesus is saying that, after we clear our vision, we can call a spade a spade. At that point, we may find that others are indeed dogs and pigs. In this context, Jesus likely has the Pharisees in mind (although the point is applicable more broadly). The Pharisees were quick to size up others and see others as beneath them (Luke 18:10–12). They were also known as hypocrites (e.g., Matt 6:2, 5, 16; 22:18; 23:13). Telling the crowd not to judge may be another way of telling them not to follow the Pharisees' example.

Followers of Jesus are not judgmental or "better than," but neither are they naïve or blind to the truth of others. Rather they are honest with themselves so they can be discerning about others.

Begin by reading aloud:

> Do not judge, or you too will be judged. For in the same way you judge others, you will be judged, and with the measure you use, it will be measured to you.
>
> Why do you look at the speck of sawdust in your brother's eye and pay no attention to the plank in your own eye? How can you say to your brother, "Let me take the speck out of your eye," when all the time there is a plank in your own eye? You hypocrite, first take the plank out of your own eye, and then you will see clearly to remove the speck from your brother's eye.

In this story, Jesus is teaching the crowd not to judge other people. It is OK when we see someone doing something wrong (like stealing) to say, "Hey. That's wrong. You should stop." That is not the kind of judging Jesus means. Jesus means we should not think we are better than other people and point out all of their faults.

In the kingdom of heaven, Jesus says there is no room for that kind of judging, where we think we are better than others. But it is so much easier to see the faults of other people than our own faults. For example, you can't always tell if you are annoying your little sister, but you sure can tell if she is annoying you! You see her faults easily, but not your own. Jesus understands that, and so he tells this story about sawdust and planks of wood to explain what to do.

Jesus says that our own faults are like a plank in our eye and the faults of others are like a little speck of dust in their eye. A plank is a wooden board, like something you might use to make a bookshelf. A plank can't really fit into your eye, and it is almost funny to picture such a thing. But imagine a board sticking out of your eye. It would be hard to see anything, right? And you certainly couldn't see something tiny like a speck of dust in someone else's eye.

Jesus is saying we should think of another person's faults not as the big problem but like a little tiny speck of wood dust in their eye that you can barely see. We should think of our own faults as huge boards sticking out of our eyes.

Before you can see someone else's faults, the tiny specks of dust in someone else's eye, Jesus says you need to take the plank out of your own eye. That means you have to be humble and honest about your own faults. Then you see the faults in others, but you won't be judging them because you know you have your own faults, too.

<table>
<tr><td>Lesson
19</td><td>Matthew 7:13–14

Living a Disciplined Life</td></tr>
</table>

What the Parent Should Know: In just two short verses, Jesus packs in a lot. He speaks of two gates, large and small, and two roads, broad and narrow. These represent the life of a disciple of Jesus. The small gate and narrow road, though more difficult to navigate, are the only choice for citizens of the kingdom.

At first blush, it might seem that this metaphor refers to salvation: to walk the road of eternal life, you need to enter through that one gate, Jesus. But reading the story this way is inconsistent with the rest of the Sermon on the Mount, where Jesus is giving instructions on how citizens of the kingdom are to live, not on how his listeners are to get saved. In fact the passages right before and after also talk about what followers <u>do</u> ("do to others what you would want them to do to you," v. 12; and "by their fruit you will recognize them," v. 20, see Lesson 20 below).

Choosing the small gate and walking on the narrow road both refer to a life of discipline—a life of self-denial and obedience in following Jesus. Being a disciple of Jesus means choosing the more difficult "road." The way to that difficult road is through a small, difficult-to-find gate. The "small gate" does not represent "Jesus." The gate, like the road, is a way of saying that the life of discipleship takes effort to "find."

The background for this is the book of Proverbs, where a road or path is a common metaphor for disciplined, wise life (e.g., Proverbs 4). Learning to live this way takes time and regular training (which is why we see the refrain in Proverbs "Listen my son.") Choosing the wide gate and broad road is easy because they require no discipline. Jesus says that an undisciplined, unwise life leads to clear, negative consequences for one's actions, as we see so often in Proverbs (13:15; 16:18; 17:19; 24:22). That is where the easy path leads.

This passage is a summary of what Jesus has been saying throughout the Sermon on the Mount: following Jesus means an inner transformation that is then lived out in daily life (see also Matthew 10:39). The two final sections of chapter seven illustrate this message: "entering the kingdom" means bearing fruit (v. 21, Lesson 20), and the "wise builder" puts into practice what Jesus says (v. 24, Year Three, Lesson 20).

Being a disciple of Jesus in the kingdom of heaven means committing oneself to following the more difficult way.

Begin by reading aloud:

> Enter through the narrow gate. For wide is the gate and broad is the road that leads to destruction, and many enter through it. But small is the gate and narrow the road that leads to life, and only a few find it.

Doing the right thing is sometimes very hard. Your parents ask you to eat your vegetables, or to stop watching TV and go outside and play in the fresh air, or finish your homework before you play a game. You may not want to do any of those things, because they are much harder to do than the fun things. But you know that your parents are probably right, and they are asking you to do these things because they love you and care about you.

In this story, Jesus is saying that being his disciple is not always easy. Sometimes a follower of Jesus needs to do things that are right even if they are hard. But just like your parents, Jesus asks you to do some hard things because he loves you and wants you to grow to love God more and more.

Jesus talks about two sizes of gates and two sizes of roads to explain that following him is not always easy. Imagine that you are in a village surrounded by a very high stone wall. The only way out is through the town gates. There are two of them. One gate is the main gate of the village. This gate is wide and tall, and you have no trouble finding it. It is the obvious gate that everyone sees. It is the easy way out. On the other side is a broad road that is easy to walk on.

The other town gate is very small and hard to find. You have to walk along the entire wall of the city, step by step, to look for it. You go right past it a couple of times without even seeing it! But finally, you find it. The doors are only a couple of feet high, and so you have to crawl on your belly to make it through. The road on the other side is narrow and you have to be careful walking on it so that you don't fall into a muddy ditch.

Even though the tall gate is easier to find and leads to a nice, wide road, that is not the way Jesus wants you to take. He wants you to take the small gate that leads to a narrow road. Jesus means that sometimes following him means having to do difficult things.

When your friend gets a brand new X-Box and the latest game that you don't have, it is easy to be jealous and even angry with him because he has something you want. That is the "wide gate and the broad road" that Jesus is talking about. That may be the easy way, but what happens if you go down that road? You become more and more angry and you may even lose a friend, all because of a game. Trouble happens when you take the easy way.

The harder road, the one Jesus wants you to take, is to not be jealous or get angry but to be content with what you have. That does not happen easily. It can take a lot of effort to stop being jealous and start being content with what you have. Grown-ups have a hard time with that, too.

Taking the small gate and the narrow road means doing what Jesus wants you to do even if it is hard. If you do what is right, even if it is hard, you will learn to know God better and better. Following Jesus is sometimes a harder road to take, but it is always the better road.

Matthew 7:15–23

Bad Trees Always Bear Bad Fruit

What the Parent Should Know: As we have seen in the previous lessons in this unit, the Sermon on the Mount has one central focus: how true disciples of Jesus are to behave as citizens of the kingdom of heaven. This passage follows that theme although it comes at it from a different angle. To borrow a contemporary proverb, "Sports don't build character, they reveal it." Jesus is saying the same thing: behavior reveals character.

Jesus makes his point by focusing on the behavior of the religious leaders and what it reveals about them. These religious leaders are false prophets (vv. 15 and 22). A prophet is not someone who predicts the future, but is a teacher, a leader, someone who speaks for God. False prophets are those who teach falsely and lead people astray. They are wolves in sheep's clothing (v. 15).

Jesus illustrates this by speaking of two types of trees in vv. 16–20: "good" trees and "bad" trees. The central point is that good and bad trees will <u>invariably</u> bear fruit consistent with what they are. The flip side of this is that a tree's fruit <u>invariably reveals</u> what kind of tree it is. There is no mystery or need for endless debate. You can tell if your leader is true or false: look at his fruit.

But what fruit does one look for to reveal truth or falsehood? Not what one might expect, things like driving out demons or performing miracles (v. 22). As great as those things are (Jesus himself did them), the fruit that reveals the nature of the tree is of another kind, namely the very things Jesus has been preaching about for the entire Sermon on the Mount: love your enemies, do not judge, give to the needy, etc. Failure to produce this fruit means the prophet is false, regardless of outward appearances.

The phrase "on that day" (v. 22) indicates that Jesus has the future in view, too. The Sermon on the Mount generally focuses on what here-and-now kingdom living looks like. But the kingdom is <u>also</u> future—it does not stop one day, but continues. Entrance into the kingdom (in the future sense) will be barred to those leaders who have not borne good fruit. These leaders think they are part of the kingdom now, but are in for a shock "on that day" when they find out they never were.

We must be careful not to draw a false conclusion. Jesus is not saying "good fruit grants one entrance to the future kingdom." He is saying that good fruit <u>reveals</u> what kind of tree one really is. The fruit does not make the tree, the tree makes the fruit. To the tree that does not bear good fruit, Jesus does not say, "Since you did not bear good fruit, I don't want you." Rather he says, "Your failure to bear good fruit indicates that I <u>never knew you</u>." No one is denied entrance to the kingdom because he doesn't "do enough," but because he is not known by Jesus.

All of this amounts to a warning to Jesus' listeners. Be careful whom you follow. Make sure they bear good fruit. If they do not bear good fruit, they are bad trees, regardless of their outward authority and reputation. They are no different than dry, useless branches that will be burned.

Begin by reading aloud:

> Watch out for false prophets. They come to you in sheep's clothing, but inwardly they are ferocious wolves. By their fruit you will recognize them. Do people pick grapes from thornbushes, or figs from thistles? Likewise every good tree bears good fruit, but a bad tree bears bad fruit. A good tree cannot bear bad fruit, and a bad tree cannot bear good fruit. Every tree that does not bear good fruit is cut down and thrown into the fire. Thus, by their fruit you will recognize them.
>
> Not everyone who says to me, "Lord, Lord," will enter the kingdom of heaven, but only he who does the will of my Father who is in heaven. Many will say to me on that day, "Lord, Lord, did we not prophesy in your name, and in your name drive out demons and perform many miracles?" Then I will tell them plainly, "I never knew you. Away from me, you evildoers!"

In this passage, Jesus talks about prophets. By "prophet," Jesus means someone who is a teacher and has authority to talk about God. Jesus calls some teachers "false prophets." These are teachers who may be very smart, but don't follow God with all their heart. A true prophet is someone who follows God, which means he loves all those around him, even enemies, and helps those in need.

The only way to tell false and true prophets apart is to watch what they do and see whether they are following Jesus. Jesus is telling his listeners, "Be careful whom you trust! Don't trust a religious leader just because he says smart things. He must also obey and follow God."

Jesus explains this with a story. False prophets are like trees that bear rotten fruit, and true prophets are like trees that bear ripe, tasty fruit. If you go outside in the spring or summer and you see an apple tree with small, rotting apples hanging from the branches—or a shade tree that is bare, with only a few brown leaves hanging on—you say to yourself, "There must be something wrong with that tree. It is either dead or sick." You can tell right away what kind of a tree it is by what grows from its branches.

And a bad tree will *always* bear bad fruit. A good tree will *always* bear good fruit. You can *always* tell the bad trees from the good. It is not a secret. You just have to look its the fruit. The same goes for the prophets Jesus is talking about: you can always tell whether the prophet is true or false by how he behaves—by his "fruit."

Jesus says that bad trees with bad fruit are cut down and thrown into the fire. Jesus means that false prophets, like bad trees with dead branches and bad fruit, are useless and good for nothing. The people should not listen to a teacher like that.

Jesus is very concerned that his listeners understand who are false prophets. He does not want the people to be fooled by them. Jesus wants the people to learn how to love God and obey him. False prophets will only lead people astray.

Lesson 20: Bad Trees Always Bear Bad Fruit

Unit 5

Jesus' Early Life

For the Parent: There are essentially three phases to Jesus' life as presented in the Gospels: the early years before his ministry begins (the topic of this unit), his ministry years (during which there is a steady movement from general acceptance to rejection of Jesus' message), and the end of his life (Passion Week). The stories of Jesus' early life are much more involved than our Christmas pageants might suggest. They are theologically loaded statements about who Jesus is, connecting him to Israel's story in the Old Testament (as can be seen most clearly in the genealogies of Matthew and Luke), and foreshadowing much of what is to follow in the Gospels. In other words, they are not a sort of picture album of Jesus' boyhood ("Oh, and here's the time the little guy wandered away from his parents.") They are setting up the story of Jesus, and so demand our attention.

Like the other units dealing with Jesus' life, this one does not try to cover every detail. Instead, certain themes are highlighted. The assumption is that this curriculum is not the student's only exposure to the basic outline of Jesus' life and ministry.

Lesson 21

God Is On the Move . . . Again

What the Parent Should Know: This story is about the angel Gabriel's announcement of John the Baptist's birth during the reign of Herod the Great, king of Judea. (Herod died in 4 BC so Jesus was born, oddly enough, BC. The Christian calendar suffers from a miscalculation on the part of some medieval monks as they tried to work out the date.) John's birth is the first indication to God's people that soon, God himself will be among them.

Gabriel gives the news to Zechariah, John's father and a priest. Zechariah and his priestly "division" are taking their turn in their temple duties. (In order to divide the labor, King David created twenty-four divisions of priests, one of which was headed by Abijah, Zechariah's ancestor.) Zechariah and his wife Elizabeth are past childbearing age, yet Gabriel (named in v. 19, meaning "mighty one of God") promises that they will have a son to be named John (meaning "The Lord is gracious"). This son will be consecrated to God's service, and so must abstain from alcohol, and he will be filled with the Spirit of God from his birth. Through his preaching John will prepare the Jews for the coming of God himself. Zechariah has trouble believing the news that he and his wife will have a child at their age, so he is struck dumb until the child's birth.

The story of John's birth is more than a mere recounting of events. The story is full of Old Testament allusions, bringing to mind the times when God was also about to do something significant for Israel. The presence of Old Testament allusions in John's birth story tells the readers: "Be alert! God is on the move again, as in the old times. He is about to do something big."

What are those allusions? John's abstinence from alcohol (v. 15; see Numbers 6:1–4) echoes similar oaths taken by Samuel (1 Samuel 1:11) and Samson (Judges 13:4–7), both of whom were set apart by God to come to Israel's aid: Samuel instituted Israel's kingship and Samson delivered the Israelites from the Philistines.

More importantly, the story of John's birth to Zechariah and Elizabeth parallels the story of Isaac's birth to Abraham and Sarah in four important ways. (1) Zechariah and Elizabeth are described as upright and blameless (v. 6, not "perfect" but scrupulous in keeping the law), as is Abraham in Genesis 17:1. (2) Both couples are past childbearing age and bear children by divine intervention. (3) Gabriel announces himself to Zechariah by say-ing, "Do not be afraid"(v. 13) as did God to Abraham in Genesis 15:1. (4) Abraham and Sarah react in disbelief at the birth announcement (Genesis 17:17 and 18:12), as does Zechariah (v. 18).

The parallel between Isaac and John also has a deeper meaning. Isaac's birth makes possible Israel's very existence several generations later (he is the father of Jacob, who is the father of the twelve tribes of Israel). The birth of John signals that God is about to do something of a similar magnitude. Through Jesus, a new "Israel" will be formed. This new people will not be limited to an Israelite ethnic identity but will be made up of both Jews and Gentiles together.

John's birth story does not simply recount events. It recalls Old Testament episodes in order to make a key point. The God of Israel is on the move once again. What is he doing now and where will it lead? That remains to be seen as Luke's Gospel unfolds.

[Note to Parents: The Old Testament allusions are central to this story, although likely too subtle for young children. In the lesson below we will focus more on the setting of the story, explain some of the detail, and introduce the parallel with Abraham and Sarah. Still, this is a good lesson for the children to begin seeing how intricately the gospel ties in to the Old Testament.]

Begin by reading aloud:

> In the time of Herod king of Judea there was a priest named Zecha-riah, who belonged to the priestly division of Abijah; his wife Eliza-beth was also a descendant of Aaron. Both of them were upright in the sight of God, observing all the Lord's commandments and regula-tions blamelessly. But they had no children, because Elizabeth was barren; and they were both well along in years.
>
> Once when Zechariah's division was on duty and he was serving as priest before God, he was chosen by lot, according to the custom of the priesthood, to go into the temple of the Lord and burn incense. And when the time for the burning of incense came, all the assembled worshipers were praying outside.
>
> Then an angel of the Lord appeared to him, standing at the right side of the altar of incense. When Zechariah saw him, he was startled and was gripped with fear. But the angel said to him: "Do not be afraid, Zechariah; your prayer has been heard. Your wife Elizabeth

will bear you a son, and you are to give him the name John. He will be a joy and delight to you, and many will rejoice because of his birth, for he will be great in the sight of the Lord. He is never to take wine or other fermented drink, and he will be filled with the Holy Spirit even from birth. Many of the people of Israel will he bring back to the Lord their God. And he will go on before the Lord, in the spirit and power of Elijah, to turn the hearts of the fathers to their children and the disobedient to the wisdom of the righteous—to make ready a people prepared for the Lord."

Zechariah asked the angel, "How can I be sure of this? I am an old man and my wife is well along in years."

The angel answered, "I am Gabriel. I stand in the presence of God, and I have been sent to speak to you and to tell you this good news. And now you will be silent and not able to speak until the day this happens, because you did not believe my words, which will come true at their proper time."

Meanwhile, the people were waiting for Zechariah and wondering why he stayed so long in the temple. When he came out, he could not speak to them. They realized he had seen a vision in the temple, for he kept making signs to them but remained unable to speak.

When his time of service was completed, he returned home. After this his wife Elizabeth became pregnant and for five months remained in seclusion. "The Lord has done this for me," she said. "In these days he has shown his favor and taken away my disgrace among the people."

In this story, the angel Gabriel tells a priest named Zechariah that he and his wife Elizabeth will have a baby, even though they are too old to have children. This baby will be named John and his job will be to teach everyone about God. All this happens during the reign of King Herod the Great. (The Romans had appointed Herod to be in charge of the land of Judea and some other territories.)

A priest was someone who worked in the temple to take care of the sacrifices that had to be made every day. Priests did things like giving blessings to people, and making sure all the furniture and lamps in the temple were in the right places and set up properly. Since there was so much work to do, the priests were divided into groups. There were twenty-four groups, and each group took care of the temple for about two weeks each year.

In this story, Zechariah's group is taking its turn working in the temple. So when Gabriel comes to Zechariah, he is at the temple, doing his job. Gabriel tells Zechariah that he and Elizabeth are going to have a baby boy. Gabriel even names the baby. Parents usually name their children, but this will not be an ordinary baby. He will grow up to be a special servant of God. So Gabriel names the baby John, which means, "The Lord is gracious." To be *gracious* is to be kind to those who don't deserve it. When John grows up he will tell everyone about how gracious God is, because everyone can be forgiven of their sins by believing in Jesus.

But Zechariah doesn't believe Gabriel, since he and Elizabeth are too old to have children. Near the very beginning of the Bible, in the book of Genesis, there is another story that sounds like the story of Zechariah and Elizabeth. It is the story of Abraham, the father of all Israel.

Like Zechariah and Elizabeth, Abraham and his wife Sarah were too old to have children, but God promised that they would have a son. Abraham and Sarah didn't believe God either, but they had a boy anyway. His name was Isaac.

Isaac's children, grandchildren, great-grandchildren, and on and on, became the nation of Israel. Without Isaac, there would have been no Israel. God did something big, back in Genesis, and it all began with one miracle baby.

John will be a miracle baby, too, just like Isaac. He too will be born to parents too old to have children. And just like Isaac, John's birth means that God is on the move again to do something grand and unexpected. This time, God is sending his son Jesus into the world to save people from their sins.

Luke 1:26–38

The Coming of the King

What the Parent Should Know: In the sixth month after John's conception, Gabriel visits Mary and tells her that she will give birth to the Son of God. His birth will bring Israel's long-awaited salvation and his reign will never end.

Mary is "highly favored" by God (vv. 28 and 30). We are not told why Mary deserves such high praise, and thoughtful readers of the Bible have been speculating ever since. But, for whatever reason, she is chosen specifically. She is engaged to Joseph, who is in the line of David, as is Mary (see Matthew 1:16), a necessary requirement for someone who will give birth to a son who will sit on David's throne. Gabriel tells Mary that the son's name will be Jesus. Matthew 1:21 explains the significance of the name: he will save his people from their sins. (Jesus is a variation of the Hebrew name Joshua, which means "salvation.") In the previous lesson, Gabriel had also announced John's name ("The Lord is gracious"). In the Old Testament, when God names a child, it indicates that the child will play some extraordinary role in God's plan (see Isaiah 7:14).

We learn from Gabriel that the boy will be called Son of the Most High, which is a way of saying that Jesus will be king. When understood from an Old Testament point of view, "Son of God" has royal connotations. Israel's kings represented God to the people; they ruled on behalf of God, and so were "sons" of God (see Psalm 2, especially v. 7). At this point, Mary is simply being told that her son will be king of Israel in the line of David, to sit on David's throne. What will make this king's reign unique is its duration. Unlike the line of David in the Old Testament, which came to a halt in the Babylonian exile (586 BC), Jesus' kingdom will not end. The perpetual line of David promised in the Old Testament (2 Samuel 7:16) will now, finally, become reality in the son of this young virgin woman.

So far, this may seem like a letdown for modern readers—"What about Jesus being God? Isn't that the real point?" We get to this in part two of Gabriel's announcement. Mary reasonably asks how she can possibly be the one to perpetuate David's line, since she is a virgin. Gabriel tells her that she will be empowered and overshadowed by the Holy Spirit, and so her son will be called "Son of God" (v. 35). Here we see the same title "Son of God" used in a second sense. It is still a royal title, recognizable to anyone at the time who knew the Old Testament. But now that title is going to be infused with extra meaning. Even though Old Testament kings represented God on earth, Jesus will take that role to a new level. This king does not represent God as the Old Testament kings did—he is "God with us" (to borrow Matthew's language in Matthew 1:23).

Israel's long wait for a king in David's line to sit once again upon his throne is now over. But this time, God himself will have a son. That son's kingdom will not end. The physical realities of the Old Testament are but shadows. With Jesus they take on a deeper meaning.

Begin by reading aloud:

                                                 Lesson 22: The Coming of the King

In the sixth month, God sent the angel Gabriel to Nazareth, a town in Galilee, to a virgin pledged to be married to a man named Joseph, a descendant of David. The virgin's name was Mary. The angel went to her and said, "Greetings, you who are highly favored! The Lord is with you."

Mary was greatly troubled at his words and wondered what kind of greeting this might be. But the angel said to her, "Do not be afraid, Mary, you have found favor with God. You will be with child and give birth to a son, and you are to give him the name Jesus. He will be great and will be called the Son of the Most High. The Lord God will give him the throne of his father David, and he will reign over the house of Jacob forever; his kingdom will never end."

"How will this be," Mary asked the angel, "since I am a virgin?"

The angel answered, "The Holy Spirit will come upon you, and the power of the Most High will overshadow you. So the holy one to be born will be called the Son of God. Even Elizabeth your relative is going to have a child in her old age, and she who was said to be barren is in her sixth month. For nothing is impossible with God."

"I am the Lord's servant," Mary answered. "May it be to me as you have said." Then the angel left her.

In this story, Mary is living in the town of Nazareth in the region of Galilee. She is engaged to be married to Joseph. The angel Gabriel—the same angel who visited Zechariah—now visits Mary to tell her she will give birth to a son. And just as Gabriel named Zechariah's son "John," he names Mary's son "Jesus." Jesus' name means "salvation." Gabriel is telling Mary that her son will bring salvation to all people. At first Mary is frightened, but then she trusts what the angel says.

Gabriel tells Mary two amazing things about the baby she will have.

First, Jesus will grow up to be king of Israel. He will sit on David's throne. You probably know who David is. He killed the giant Goliath with a slingshot and became the king of the nation of Israel. He was not perfect, but he loved God. He tried to be a just king and follow God's law. As long as a king like David was ruling the Israelites, they knew that God was with them. The Israelites hoped that David's son, and grandson, and great-grandson (and on and on) would be just like David and be good kings.

But David's sons and grandsons did not love and follow God as David did. Instead they disobeyed God. This went on for about 500 years until God sent a foreign nation called the Babylonians to conquer Israel. The

Babylonians destroyed Israel's palace and the temple, stole Israel's treasure, killed some of Israel's rulers, and took a lot of the Israelites with them back to Babylon as captives. That was the end of any son of David sitting on the throne.

When Jesus was born, Israel had been without a king like David for a long time—about 600 years. They were hoping that one day soon a king like David would rule over them—someone who loved God and loved the people. Gabriel tells Mary that her son Jesus will be that king.

Second, Gabriel tells Mary that Jesus will be different from every other king Israel ever had. David's kingdom came to end when the Babylonians came, but Gabriel says that Jesus' kingdom won't come to an end. Why? Because Jesus is God's Son. God sent his Son Jesus to be the king forever.

This story does not talk about all the things that Jesus will do and say when he grows up. It doesn't talk about Jesus dying on the cross or rising from the dead, either. Right now all Gabriel is doing is telling Mary that her baby Jesus is the king everyone has been waiting for.

Lesson 23

Luke 1:39–56

God Exalts the Humble

What the Parent Should Know: After Gabriel's announcement to Mary (Lesson 22), she visits her relative Elizabeth (Elizabeth may have been Mary's cousin, but that is not certain). John leaps in Elizabeth's womb when Mary greets her. Elizabeth, filled with the Holy Spirit, has a moment of insight: Mary and the child are blessed by God.

Mary answers Elizabeth with a prayer of praise often called the Magnificat. This word means "glorifies" and it is the first word of this passage in the Latin translation of the Bible (the Vulgate). In this prayer, Mary glorifies God for making her the vessel through which God will come to the aid of his people.

Many reading this passage today, knowing something about where the story of Jesus is headed, might be surprised to see that Mary's prayer does not talk about Jesus coming to save the world from sin. The key to understanding this prayer is to pay attention to its Old Testament background. The heart of Mary's prayer is praise to God for his faithfulness in exalting those in humble circumstances, which means both Mary herself (v. 48) and Israel as a nation (v. 52). Mary is in humble circumstances because she is a young woman. Women in general were socially powerless, and a young woman like Mary (possibly no older than fourteen) was wholly subject to her parents. Israel is also humbled because Israel is God's people, yet under the thumb of Roman rule.

The Old Testament background is the prayer of Hannah in 1 Samuel 2:1–11. In fact, Mary's prayer is meant to remind us of Hannah's. Hannah was barren and God exalted her by giving her a son with her husband Elkanah. Her son Samuel then became a prophet and oversaw Israel's transition from being ruled by judges to being judged by kings. So, the birth of Samuel exalted Hannah, who had been humbled by her childless state, because she was no longer barren. His birth also would exalt Israel nationally. Up to that time, Israel had not been a nation but a collection of twelve tribes, often in conflict with each other. Having a king united them, and gave them nation status on a par with the other nations.

Like Samuel, Jesus will exalt Israel. Now finally God is coming to help Israel and to be merciful to Abraham's descendants (vv. 54–55). Jesus will sit on the throne of David in order to humble the proud (Israel's oppressors) and exalt the humble (Jewish residents of Judea, guests of the Romans in their own land; vv. 50–53).

The first chapter of Luke, as a whole, presents Jesus as the one who fulfills Israel's nationalistic hope for a king who will exalt them from their present humility—an almost forgotten rump state within the mighty Roman Empire. This king will rule with justice, righteousness, and mercy. What is not yet expressed in this prayer is that Jesus' kingdom will move far beyond the boundaries of Israel. As will we see throughout the Gospels, Jesus' kingdom will include Israel, but will not be limited to Israel.

Begin by reading aloud:

At that time Mary got ready and hurried to a town in the hill country of Judea, where she entered Zechariah's home and greeted Elizabeth. When Elizabeth heard Mary's greeting, the baby leaped in her womb, and Elizabeth was filled with the Holy Spirit. In a loud voice she exclaimed: "Blessed are you among women, and blessed is the child you will bear! But why am I so favored, that the mother of my Lord should come to me? As soon as the sound of your greeting reached my ears, the baby in my womb leaped for joy. Blessed is she who has believed that what the Lord has said to her will be accomplished!"

And Mary said:

> "My soul glorifies the Lord and my spirit rejoices in God my
>   Savior,
> for he has been mindful of the humble state of his servant.
> From now on all generations will call me blessed, for the Mighty
>   One has done great things for me—holy is his name.
> His mercy extends to those who fear him, from generation to
>   generation.
> He has performed mighty deeds with his arm; he has scattered
>   those who are proud in their inmost thoughts.
> He has brought down rulers from their thrones but has lifted
>   up the humble.
> He has filled the hungry with good things but has sent the rich
>   away empty.
> He has helped his servant Israel, remembering to be merciful
>   to Abraham and his descendants forever, even as he said
>   to our fathers."

Mary stayed with Elizabeth for about three months and then returned home.

After Mary learns from the angel Gabriel that she is going to have a baby, she hurries to visit her relative Elizabeth. (Elizabeth may have been Mary's cousin, aunt, or some other relative. We don't know exactly.) Elizabeth already knew that she was going to have a baby, too, John the Baptist.

When Mary greets Elizabeth, right then Elizabeth feels her baby moving and kicking inside of her. Elizabeth understands this is not just a normal baby kick. God is telling Elizabeth that her baby and Mary's baby are both blessed by God. Both Mary and Mary's child are going to be used by God in some extraordinary way. Mary already knows this because Gabriel told her, but now Elizabeth knows too, and she tells Mary so.

Then Mary praises God because he has given her the honor to be the mother of King Jesus. Mary did not expect this. After all, Mary is a very young and very poor woman. There is nothing at all exceptional about her. She is not powerful, famous, or important. Mary is amazed that God would choose someone like her to be the mother of Jesus. That is why she sings this song about how joyful she is that God has given her this honor.

Lesson 23: God Exalts the Humble

Mary knows that God is also doing a great thing for Israel. She praises God for that, too. Like Mary, Israel is also lowly and humble and needs God's help. In what way is Israel lowly and humble? The powerful Romans have taken over Israel's country and are ruling over the Jews—in their own land!

Imagine if your family went on a long vacation for a month, and then you came home and another family had moved into your house. As soon as you walked in you would be told where to sleep, when to eat, when you could watch TV, when to go to bed. You would have no more freedom in your own house. That would be humiliating and probably make you angry. How dare these people just walk into your house and take over!

That is what it was like to be an Israelite in the days of Mary. The Israelites lived in their own land, but the Romans ran it. The Israelites longed for the day when God would give them a king who would let them have their land back. That way they could have a king, a son of David, sitting on the throne—not a king picked for them by the Romans.

Now, Mary understands that Jesus will be the king who will help lowly and humble Israel. But Mary does not yet understand that Jesus is not just going to be Israel's king. Jesus' kingdom is the kingdom of heaven, and it will stretch far beyond Israel. His kingdom will be made up of people who love God and try to follow what Jesus teaches. Mary does not understand that yet but she will soon.

Lesson 24

Luke 1:57–80

God is about to Rescue Israel

What the Parent Should Know: Eight days after John the Baptist's birth, he was circumcised according to the Law of Moses (Leviticus 12:3) and named. It was customary to name the child after the father or someone in the family, so the people present objected when Elizabeth announced that his name would be John. She was following Gabriel's instruction, which no one but she and Zechariah knew about (v. 13). Zechariah reinforces Elizabeth's words by writing on a tablet "His name is John," at which point Zechariah is able to speak again.

The heart of this passage is the prophecy of Zechariah that follows (vv. 67–79). Zechariah understands that John's birth is the first in a series of events for Israel that will lead to redemption and salvation—the hope of many centuries of God's people (vv. 68–69). He also understands the role that his son is going to play in preparing the way for God's work. For these things he praises God. The commonly used Latin title for Zechariah's prophecy is Benedictus, *which is the Latin translation (the Vulgate) of the opening words "Blessed be."*

So, what exactly is God doing that is so praiseworthy? Some of the same things we saw in Mary's prayer. The birth of John shows that God "has come and redeemed his people" Israel (v. 68). Note the use of the past tense: with the birth of John, the redemption of Israel has begun even if it is not yet complete. John's birth is the first stage of redemption, and Jesus' birth will be the second.

But what does Zechariah mean by "redemption"? We have seen throughout Luke 1 that the Jews were counting on God to be faithful to them by putting a king on David's throne—to give them political and religious freedom. To use Zechariah's words, God will once again "raise up a horn of salvation" in David's house, to deliver the people "from the hand of all who hate us" (vv. 69–71; "horn" is a symbol of strength, like the horn of an animal—see Deuteronomy 33:17; Psalms 18:2; 75:4–5, 10). John's birth indicates that God is now starting to bring all this about.

John will "prepare the way" for God to act (v. 76): God is coming to bring "salvation" to God's people, to "forgive their sins," and show them "tender mercy." The Old Testament used language like this when God delivered the Israelites from the Babylonian exile. In Isaiah 40:1–5, God says that Israel's national troubles were the result of their national sin of disobedience to God's law. The Jews of Jesus' time likewise understood their present political woes (Roman occupation) as continued punishment for their own sin. They were waiting for God to come again, forgive their sins, save them, and be merciful to them.

God is indeed on the move, as Zechariah prophesies, but not in the way Zechariah could grasp at the moment. Yes, God is coming, but not as a warring king taking vengeance on his enemies. He will come as the child of peasants. Jesus will speak of God's love, God's forgiveness, and tender mercy. He will teach the people that the problem they face is much deeper than captivity by the Romans. Jesus' mission is to release everyone—Jew and Gentile—from their sins so they can know God fully.

This passage is a wonderful example of how Jesus fulfills the Old Testament: Jesus does not simply meet Old Testament expectations but moves beyond them and transforms them.

                              Lesson 24: God is about to Rescue Israel

[Note to Parents: The biblical text speaks of circumcision, but that is left out here in case you are not ready to explain this to your child, or in case you are teaching a group. If you do decide to explain circumcision, you may simply say that it was a Jewish custom rooted in the command given to Abraham in Genesis 17. In Jewish custom, naming the child coincided with circumcision on the eighth day.]

Begin by reading aloud:

When it was time for Elizabeth to have her baby, she gave birth to a son. Her neighbors and relatives heard that the Lord had shown her great mercy, and they shared her joy.

On the eighth day they came to circumcise the child, and they were going to name him after his father Zechariah, but his mother spoke up and said, "No! He is to be called John."

They said to her, "There is no one among your relatives who has that name."

Then they made signs to his father, to find out what he would like to name the child. He asked for a writing tablet, and to everyone's astonishment he wrote, "His name is John." Immediately his mouth was opened and his tongue was loosed, and he began to speak, praising God. The neighbors were all filled with awe, and throughout the hill country of Judea people were talking about all these things. Everyone who heard this wondered about it, asking, "What then is this child going to be?" For the Lord's hand was with him.

His father Zechariah was filled with the Holy Spirit and prophesied:

> "Praise be to the Lord, the God of Israel, because he has come
> and has redeemed his people.
> He has raised up a horn of salvation for us in the house of his
> servant David (as he said through his holy prophets of long
> ago), salvation from our enemies and from the hand of all
> who hate us—
> to show mercy to our fathers and to remember his holy cov-
> enant, the oath he swore to our father Abraham:
> to rescue us from the hand of our enemies, and to enable us
> to serve him without fear in holiness and righteousness
> before him all our days.
> And you, my child, will be called a prophet of the Most High; for
> you will go on before the Lord to prepare the way for him,

to give his people the knowledge of salvation through the for-
    giveness of their sins,
because of the tender mercy of our God, by which the rising
    sun will come to us from heaven
to shine on those living in darkness and in the shadow of death,
to guide our feet into the path of peace."

And the child grew and became strong in spirit; and he lived in the desert until he appeared publicly to Israel.

It is finally time for John the Baptist to be born. Elizabeth is too old to have children, but God has given her a baby anyway. Elizabeth and her friends are filled with joy.

In this story John is eight days old and his parents Elizabeth and Zechariah are ready to name him. Everyone thinks that Zechariah and Elizabeth are going to name the baby after the father, or at least after another relative. That was the custom back then. But Elizabeth says, "No, his name is to be John" even though no relative has that name. John is what the angel Gabriel told Zechariah to name the baby.

Everyone thinks Elizabeth is making a mistake naming the baby John, so they try to find out what Zechariah wants to name the baby. You may remember from another story that Zechariah has not been able to talk ever since Gabriel visited him almost a year earlier. When Gabriel told Zechariah that he and Elizabeth would have a baby in their old age, Zechariah did not believe him. Gabriel said: "Since you don't believe this good news I am giving you, you won't be able to talk until the baby is born." So, when Zechariah is asked what he wants to name the boy, he has to write his answer on a tablet. Zechariah writes, "His name is John." Right away, Zechariah is able to speak again.

Now that Zechariah can finally talk, all he wants to do is tell everyone there that God is about to rescue his people. For many years, the Jews had been ruled by the Romans. Even though the Jews were living in their own land that God gave them, they still had to do what the Romans said. The Jews were waiting for God to come and rescue them from the Romans, but they did not know when this would happen.

Zechariah understands that the birth of John is a sign from God that God is about to rescue the Jews. Zechariah hopes that now finally a powerful king will come to defeat the Romans.

Zechariah is right that God is coming to rescue the people, but not in the way Zechariah thinks. God is not going to send a king with an army who will start a war to save Israel. Instead, God is going to rescue the people in another way. God is sending his son, Jesus, to save everyone from their sins. Zechariah does not understand that yet—but soon enough he will.

Jesus' Disciples

For the Parent: The identity of Jesus' disciples, and the types of exchanges Jesus had with them, give us yet another angle from which to understand who Jesus was and what he did. The fact that there were twelve disciples is not random, but a clear echo of the twelve tribes of Israel. The very fact that Jesus had disciples at all is itself a theological statement: Jesus is starting up a "new Israel," the kingdom of God/heaven, although this one will ultimately be made up of Jews and Gentiles and will not be founded on the Mosaic Law. One might say that the disciples were the first citizens of this new kingdom. This whole notion of Jesus and the new Israel follows nicely on the previous lessons on Jesus' early life, where Matthew especially makes this very point—that Jesus is bringing a new kingdom, a new "version," as it were, of Israel.

It is also encouraging for us to see the extent to which Jesus' closest followers simply keep missing the point of his words and actions. Jesus' message, although very much tied to Israel's story in the Old Testament, was also fresh and to a certain extent unexpected. It had to be taught patiently, over a three-year period of Jesus' public ministry, and was not given its clearest expression until Easter and Pentecost. If even Jesus' hand-picked disciples required such an extended education to catch on, we should not be surprised if the message of Jesus sometimes requires effort on our part to comprehend.

<table><tr><td>**Lesson**
25</td></tr></table>

Jesus is the Son of God

What the Parent Should Know: While traveling in the region of the Sea of Galilee (15:29), Jesus and his disciples come to Caesarea Philippi, a city north of Galilee. (Another city called Caesarea was much larger and located along the Mediterranean Sea.) There, Peter puts into words a great truth: Jesus' true identity is Israel's final anointed king, the true Son of God. No one else recognizes this yet—and Peter himself only comes to this conclusion through divine insight.

Jesus asks his disciples who people say the "Son of Man" is. Jesus frequently refers to himself as the "Son of Man" in the Gospels. The phrase comes from Daniel 7:13–14, where "one like a son of man" is endowed by God with authority and power, and whose reign will not end (see v. 14). By itself, the phrase "son of man" simply means "human being," so in Daniel "one like a son of man" means "someone who looks human but clearly is much more." By Jesus' day, the phrase "Son of Man" had come to be a shorthand way of referring to Daniel 7:13–14 as a whole. In other words it became a messianic title. So, Jesus is asking his disciples whether others understand that he is the Messiah.

Peter answers that the people have all sorts of ideas about who Jesus is, but they do not think he is Israel's Messiah. Instead, many who have listened to Jesus think that he is one of the dead prophets come back to life: John the Baptist, Elijah, or Jeremiah. Why these three? Like Jesus, John and Jeremiah had also been highly critical of the religious authorities. (In fact, in 14:1–12, Herod thought that Jesus was John the Baptist, raised from the dead.) And Elijah was a miracle worker like Jesus.

These popular perceptions are reasonable. Peter's answer, however, is that Jesus is not John or an Old Testament prophet come back to life, but "the Christ, the Son of the living God."

Peter's confession has a dual meaning. On one level, "Christ" and "Son of God" are royal titles used of human kings. "Christ" is Greek for "anointed" (as is the Hebrew word "messiah"). All of Israel's kings were "anointed ones" because royal status was conferred upon them through anointing by oil. Likewise "Son of God" is an Old Testament royal title, as we see in Psalm 2:7. Peter's confession of Jesus reflects what the disciples as a whole understood

Jesus to be: <u>the</u> long-awaited king who will rid the land of Israel's enemies and usher in a new era of peace, blessing, and above all faithfulness to God on the part of the Jews.

On another level, Peter's confession of Jesus proclaims his divinity. Jesus is more than any messiah that the Jews at the time were expecting, and Peter's insight is so profound that it can only given to Peter by divine revelation. In fact, without him realizing it, Peter's confession of Jesus is the foundational, bedrock truth upon which the entire church is built. ("Church" is used only here and in Matthew 18:17 in all of the Gospels, and it is another way of saying "kingdom of God" or "kingdom of heaven.")

Jesus declares Peter to be the "rock" (a play on the name Peter, which means rock in Greek). Upon this rock, Jesus says he will build his church. Peter's confession of Jesus as the coming king is the foundational truth upon which the church exists. Without this understanding of who Jesus is, there is no foundation upon which to build, which means there is no church.

There is even more to Peter's confession. Jesus adds, even the "gates of Hades" will not overcome the kingdom of God, this church built on the solid foundation. Hades is the abode of the dead, and the "gates of Hades" refers to the power of death, the ultimate, menacing spiritual enemy. Jesus does not fill in the details here, but later his disciples will learn that the defeat of death is the result of King Jesus rising from the dead.

Finally, Jesus says that Peter is given the "keys of the kingdom of heaven." The popular notion is of Saint Peter standing at the Pearly Gates of heaven deciding who may and who may not enter the blessed afterlife. But, as we have seen, "kingdom of heaven" is not a picture of the afterlife but of the presence and power of God here on earth through his people.

Nevertheless, what this phrase means precisely has challenged biblical interpreters for centuries. Roman Catholics understand this to mean that Peter is the first pope, whose decisions have absolute authority. Protestants have had several views. Some believe that this implies biblical infallibility. Others think this refers to Pentecost, where Peter opens up the kingdom to all who believe. Still others interpret this as individual churches exercising discipline of their members.

All believers, though, can agree on the heart of this passage: Peter's confession that Jesus is the Son of God is foundational for the building of the kingdom of God. No power will be able to stand in the way of this kingdom. For now, however, Jesus tells the disciples to stay quiet about all of this. Given the tense climate, an open declaration that Jesus was the "Christ" would be misunderstood as open political rebellion. As Jesus explains in the passage, such a kingdom is the furthest thing from Jesus' mind.

In this story, Jesus and his disciples have just crossed the Sea of Galilee. Jesus has just finished feeding four thousand people with only seven loaves of bread and a few fish. Now, Jesus and his disciples have gotten out of the boat and are traveling across the land near the Sea of Galilee. As the story begins, they have just come to the city Caesarea Philippi.

> When Jesus came to the region of Caesarea Philippi, he asked his disciples, "Who do people say the Son of Man is?"
>
> They replied, "Some say John the Baptist; others say Elijah; and still others, Jeremiah or one of the prophets."
>
> "But what about you?" he asked. "Who do you say I am?"
>
> Simon Peter answered, "You are the Christ, the Son of the living God."
>
> Jesus replied, "Blessed are you, Simon son of Jonah, for this was not revealed to you by man, but by my Father in heaven. And I tell you that you are Peter, and on this rock I will build my church, and the gates of Hades will not overcome it. I will give you the keys of the kingdom of heaven; whatever you bind on earth will be bound in heaven, and whatever you loose on earth will be loosed in heaven."
>
> Then he warned his disciples not to tell anyone that he was the Christ.

Jesus has been teaching people about God for approximately two years, and he wants to see whether they really understand that he is the Son of God. Jesus asks Peter what he has been hearing from the people.

Peter says that some people think Jesus is John the Baptist. John the Baptist used to criticize the leaders the same way Jesus does. Others think Jesus is Elijah. Elijah was an Old Testament prophet who performed miracles—like healings—just like Jesus. Others think Jesus is another Old Testament prophet, Jeremiah. Jeremiah used to tell the priests and kings of his day that God would punish them if they did not obey God. Jesus says the same thing to the religious leaders of his day.

But the people are wrong. Jesus is not John the Baptist, Elijah, or Jeremiah. So Jesus asks whether Peter and the other disciples understand who he is. Peter answers, "You are the Christ, the Son of the living God." "Christ" means "anointed." All of Israel's kings were anointed by oil when they began their rule. Peter says that Jesus is the king, but not like all of Israel's other kings. Jesus is God's own Son. That is the right answer. Jesus is not John the Baptist, Elijah, or Jeremiah. Jesus is God's Son.

When Peter gives the right answer, Jesus says to him, "You are the rock and on that rock I will build my church." (Jesus usually says "kingdom of God," but here he says "church." They mean the same thing.) Jesus calls Peter the rock because "Peter" means "rock" in their language, Greek. But Jesus also calls Peter the rock because what Peter says about Jesus is like a solid foundation for a building.

Today when builders build a house, they begin with a solid foundation made of concrete. Without a foundation, the house will fall over as soon as there is a storm—or even a strong wind. In Jesus' day there was no concrete, so when builders put up very large buildings, like temples or palaces, they always constructed them on a flat hard surface—a rock—so that the building wouldn't fall down later.

When Peter says that Jesus is the Son of God, that is like the foundation of a building. Everyone else who follows Jesus must also understand Jesus is the Son of God, just like Peter and the first disciples. So, the disciples are like a foundation, and the others who come later and *also* believe that Jesus is the Christ and the Son of God are like a building built on top of that foundation.

Jesus' kingdom is like a building on a solid rock than no one can knock down. Jesus says that his kingdom is even stronger than death. In this story, Jesus calls death the "gates of Hades." Later, Jesus' disciples will learn exactly what Jesus means here. After he is crucified, Jesus will rise from the dead. And Jesus promises that his followers will also rise from the dead when Jesus comes back again.

<table>
<tr><td>Lesson
26</td><td align="right">Matthew 18:1–4
No One Has a Higher Rank
in God's Kingdom</td></tr>
</table>

What the Parent Should Know: After another round of doing battle with the religious leaders (17:24–27), Jesus and his disciples have a moment to themselves. The disciples take the opportunity to ask Jesus who is greatest in the kingdom of heaven. But they do not get the answer they are expecting. Instead they discover that the question itself is out of bounds, for in Jesus' kingdom there is no rank.

It's natural enough for the disciples to ask about rank. They are in on the ground floor of something big, so to speak, and so they begin thinking of benefits that stem from their situation: "Who is the greatest in the kingdom of heaven?" They may be asking about how they rank among themselves ("Who is second in command behind you, Jesus?"), or whether they will all rank above the other followers of Jesus, those not part of the inner circle of disciples.

Either way, this is the wrong question to ask. The disciples still do not seem to understand that the "kingdom of heaven" is not the reign of a military messiah who will retake Jerusalem and rid the land of the Roman oppressors. The kingdom Jesus announces in his preaching and miracles is not one of armed conquest but forgiveness of sins and inner transformation by the Spirit that works itself out in everyday living.

Members of this kingdom are marked by humility, and so questions of rank are completely out of place. To demonstrate this, Jesus puts a child in front of them. The child represents humility (v. 4), which does not refer to a humble disposition but being in a powerless position in society. Children have no rank in earthly kingdoms—no power or status, no place in a hierarchy. The kingdom of heaven is made up of those who are in such humble positions—not those who hold some rank, but rather those who have no rank at all.

The kingdom of heaven upsets all conventional expectations, including those of Jesus' closest followers. They want to know who is greatest in the kingdom. But Jesus answers that unless they remove all such questions of rank from their thinking and become like a status-less, humble child, they won't even <u>enter</u> that kingdom (v. 3).

[Note to Parents: As we have seen in other lessons, "entering" the kingdom of heaven does not mean "going to heaven when you die." Jesus means that those who think of rank have no place in the kingdom Jesus is building here and now. Eternal destiny is not the topic here.]

Begin by reading aloud:

> At that time the disciples came to Jesus and asked, "Who is the greatest in the kingdom of heaven?"
>
> He called a little child and had him stand among them. And he said: "I tell you the truth, unless you change and become like little children, you will never enter the kingdom of heaven. Therefore, whoever humbles himself like this child is the greatest in the kingdom of heaven."

Jesus' twelve disciples were handpicked by Jesus. He chose not the powerful people of the world, but people like fishermen and tax collectors. These disciples follow Jesus all over as he tells people about God. No one else is as close to Jesus as the twelve disciples.

Even though they all came from humble places to start with, the disciples begin to think that they are just below Jesus in authority and higher than everyone else. In this story, Jesus teaches them that no one is higher than anyone else in his kingdom.

The disciples think that following Jesus is like being in an army. In an army, officers have different ranks, or positions of authority and power. The higher the rank, the more power an officer has. In the United States Army, the officer with the highest rank is known as the general. Under the general are other officers. First come colonels, then majors, then captains, and then lieutenants. Generals have the most power of any army officer—and lieutenants have the least.

The disciples of Jesus want to have higher rank than any other followers of Jesus. That is why they ask Jesus, "Who is the greatest in your kingdom?" They are asking, "Do we get to be generals in your kingdom?" The disciples hope that they will have power and authority over others of lower rank. They hope that other believers in Jesus will be treated more like captains—or lieutenants.

But the disciples have it all wrong. Even though Jesus picked the disciples, they do not rank higher than anyone else. In Jesus' kingdom, there is no rank at all.

Jesus decides to show the disciples exactly what this means. So he calls a small child over and tells the disciples, "If you want to be my disciple you have to be like this small child." Children don't have any power or authority. They are usually told by adults what they need to do. And children certainly have no rank in kingdoms or armies.

Jesus teaches the disciples that in his kingdom, everyone is like a small child. No one has more power or less power than anyone else. No one has a higher or lower rank. Everyone is following God together. If the disciples want to be a part of the kingdom of heaven, they will have to forget all about where they rank.

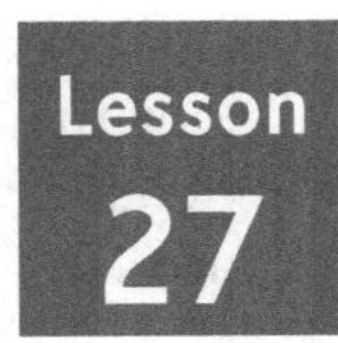

Jesus Leaves No One Out

What the Parent Should Know: Immediately before this passage, in Mark 9:33–37, Mark gives a shorter version of the "who is the greatest" episode that we saw in Lesson 26 (Matthew 18:1–6). In this lesson, Mark follows with another exchange about the disciples and their status. The disciples are fretting about "outsiders," those not part of Jesus' inner circle. Here Jesus teaches them that talk of "insiders" and "outsiders" is completely foreign to the kingdom of God. Everyone who does deeds of service toward others in Christ's name is an insider, even if not part of Jesus' inner circle like the disciples are.

The scene is set when the disciples see an "outsider" performing miracles in Jesus' name. Apparently the disciples believed that only they should have the privilege of doing impressive miracles such as driving out demons (vs. 38). It is natural for people, once they feel they are in a position of power and status, to be reluctant to let others take part. Such an attitude can quickly encourage an "us vs. them" mentality, which is clearly at work with the disciples.

Wanting to be an insider and protect one's status may be normal human behavior, but it is not kingdom behavior. The disciples rebuked the "outsider" for performing a service of mercy in Jesus' name, and they evidently felt that Jesus was going to approve of their behavior. But they quickly saw that Jesus did not share their exclusive view of discipleship.

For Jesus, anyone who does merciful acts like this in his name is an insider. To do something in the name of another means to act on behalf of that person, to represent him and place yourself under his authority. That is what this "outsider" was doing. By doing acts in Jesus' name, he was automatically included in the same circle of those who believe in Jesus, and Jesus welcomes him as if he is one of the Twelve.

And for Jesus, big acts of mercy are not what makes one a disciple. Little things—in fact inconspicuous things like giving a drink of water to another who "belongs" to Christ (v. 41)—qualify one to be part of Jesus' inner circle.

No one who does these deeds of mercy in the name of Jesus is excluded from his inner circle. It does not matter if the disciples know them, are familiar with them, or recognize them. They belong. Jesus' teaching here applies to any type of "border protection" today among Christians. Any thinking that considers any one denomination, church, or theological tradition as closer to

Jesus' inner circle is making the same mistake the disciples made. All today who genuinely desire to follow Christ and are doing the things he commanded are part of his inner circle. And any point of view that is quick to draw lines and put others on the "outside" does not belong in the kingdom.

[Note to Parents: Demon possession is a state of deep psychological torment brought on by supernatural forces. This is a very difficult—and frightening—issue for young children to comprehend. So, we will not draw attention to it in the children's lesson. We recommend to parents not to draw undue attention to this one part of the passage and focus rather on the issue of insiders and outsiders, which is such a powerful dimension of this passage in particular and Jesus' preaching as a whole. If your child asks what demon possession is and you are unsure how to answer, you might say, "People who were demon-possessed were being tormented by spiritual forces they couldn't control." It is common—and unnecessary—for a young child to worry that this is something that might happen to him, so you might also say, "You belong to God, so this can't happen to you."]

Begin by reading aloud:

"Teacher," said John, "we saw a man driving out demons in your name and we told him to stop, because he was not one of us."

"Do not stop him," Jesus said. "No one who does a miracle in my name can in the next moment say anything bad about me, for whoever is not against us is for us. Truly I tell you, anyone who gives you a cup of water in my name because you belong to the Messiah will certainly not lose their reward."

Jesus tells the disciples that anyone who does miracles in his name also belongs to Jesus—not just the twelve disciples.

What does Jesus mean when he says that these other people are doing things "in Jesus' name"? Think of a king who sends out one of his messengers to a distant part of the kingdom to deliver a message to a nobleman. The messenger arrives at the castle and knocks on the wooden gates and says "Open up *in the name of the king.*" That means the nobleman needs to open up the door as if the king himself were knocking.

The person Jesus is talking about in this story is like this messenger. Even though he is not one of the twelve disciples, he is following King Jesus and doing his bidding, just like the disciples are.

But the disciples don't like this and try to stop him. The disciples have been with Jesus from the beginning. They have seen him do all sorts of miracles to help people. But now the disciples see someone else who claims to be following Jesus and is doing miracles in Jesus' name. How could that be? They don't know this person. This person isn't with Jesus every day like the disciples are. Who does he think he is?

The disciples think that following Jesus is like joining a secret club where only a few people are let in and everyone else is left out. Has that ever happened to you? Have you ever been left out when a group of kids is going to a party or up to a tree house? It feels terrible not to belong. Jesus is teaching his disciples that the kingdom of God is not like a secret club where only a few people belong. All those who want follow Jesus and obey him are equal.

Jesus also tells the disciples that you don't have to do big things in his name to show that you belong to Jesus. Even small acts of kindness done in Jesus' name count—like giving someone a cold drink of water. Whatever you do for others in Jesus' name matters to Jesus—big things or small things.

So, who is a disciple of Jesus? Not just the twelve disciples who walked and talked with Jesus, but anyone who tries to obey Jesus and do what he says. There is no secret club where only a few people get to follow Jesus. Jesus keeps no one on the outside.

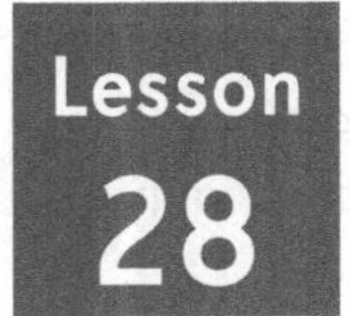

Lesson 28

Mark 10:35–45
Jesus' Followers Are Servants, not Commanders

What the Parent Should Know: The final lesson of this unit deals with another passage about the disciples' preoccupation with their status in Jesus' kingdom. In Lesson 25, we saw that Peter's confession of Jesus as "the Christ, the Son of the living God" sets him (and the disciples) apart from all others as the rock upon which Jesus will build his church. But whereas Jesus exalts the disciples one moment, he is also quick to remind them that there is no privileged status for them. The disciples have not yet come to terms with this paradox, as we have seen in Lessons 26 and 27.

Here in Lesson 28, we continue this theme: two brothers speak openly of wanting to share Jesus' power and authority, and hope to elevate their status over that of the other disciples. Jesus tolerates this discussion briefly before chiding all of the disciples for failing to grasp that his kingdom is about serving, not leading.

Jesus and the disciples are on their way up to Jerusalem, the capital. Jesus has just finished explaining to the Twelve that he will be betrayed, humiliated, and crucified—and then rise three days later (10:32–34). Apparently the sons of Zebedee, James and John, either are not listening very well, simply do not understand what Jesus means, or are hypnotized by the sight of the capital and the thought of taking over and coming into power.

So, oblivious to Jesus' speech, the brothers take Jesus aside and request of him the privilege of sitting on the left and right side of Jesus in his "glory." "Left" and "right" are metaphors for positions of power (the "right hand" being second in command, see for example Psalm 110:1). The brothers are not thinking of Jesus ruling from on high after his resurrection. Rather, they picture Jesus sitting on the throne of Jerusalem, and themselves ruling beside him. Clearly, these two disciples still do not understand that the kingdom of heaven that Jesus preached had no earthly throne or prestigious positions. They also do not understand that Jesus, far from being a powerful earthly king, would be condemned, mocked, spit on, flogged, and killed (v. 33).

Jesus responds somewhat curtly, "You don't know what you're asking" (v. 38). Jesus was destined to "drink the cup" and be "baptized," which are metaphors referring to his suffering and death. (Drinking the cup is a potent Old Testament metaphor for absorbing God's full anger. For example, in Isaiah 51:17, Israel drained the cup of God's wrath to its dregs during the exile in Babylon.) Jesus is asking the brothers whether they really think they can share in his fate.

The brothers, without skipping a beat, answer that they can certainly share in Jesus' fate, but they still do not understand what Jesus' fate will be; they are just saying, "Yeah, yeah, sure—just give us the power." Jesus tells them that they will indeed share his cup and baptism, meaning they too will eventually suffer persecution. Positions of authority, however, are not his to give. These are things that are "prepared" (by God) and so out of Jesus' control. Jesus is clearly not interested in pursuing this line of thought with James and John.

The brothers have tried to gain some advantage over the other disciples, and when the others catch on, they are angry. (Anyone ever caught in a "political" struggle at work or church can easily identify with the emotions that must have flying about.) Jesus' response to all the disciples is simple yet unsettling and powerful. He does not tell the brothers to leave the group for their politicking. (Actually, judging by the reaction of the other ten, they were all guilty of thinking in terms of rankings, for why else would they be so upset?) Rather, Jesus brings the whole group together and ends the discussion entirely. "You are ALL wrong. There is no power and authority in my kingdom. That's how earthly kingdoms operate, but in my kingdom, being great means being a servant and slave. Look at me: I am the Son of Man, but I am here to serve—to die."

Following King Jesus means all thoughts of power, authority, and rank dissipate. To be a disciple of Jesus is to lead a life of service where you consider others more highly than yourself. This attitude was as counter-intuitive then as it is now. Yet, that is what life in the kingdom of heaven is all about.

Begin by reading aloud:

Then James and John, the sons of Zebedee, came to him. "Teacher," they said, "we want you to do for us whatever we ask."

"What do you want me to do for you?" he asked.

They replied, "Let one of us sit at your right and the other at your left in your glory."

"You don't know what you are asking," Jesus said. "Can you drink the cup I drink or be baptized with the baptism I am baptized with?"

"We can," they answered.

Jesus said to them, "You will drink the cup I drink and be baptized with the baptism I am baptized with, but to sit at my right or left is not for me to grant. These places belong to those for whom they have been prepared."

When the ten heard about this, they became indignant with James and John. Jesus called them together and said, "You know that those who are regarded as rulers of the Gentiles lord it over them, and their high officials exercise authority over them. Not so with you. Instead, whoever wants to become great among you must be your servant, and whoever wants to be first must be slave of all. For even the Son of Man did not come to be served, but to serve, and to give his life as a ransom for many."

Jesus and his disciples are on their way to Jerusalem. Soon Jesus will enter Jerusalem to be crucified. On the way, he teaches the disciples a lesson: following Jesus means serving one another, not having power over each other.

          Lesson 28: Jesus' Followers Are Servants, not Commanders

On the way to Jerusalem, Jesus reminds the disciples that he will be crucified there and then rise from the dead three days later. He is preparing them for what will happen a week or so later. Even though Jesus keeps telling his disciples that he will be crucified, some of them still think that Jesus is going to Jerusalem to fight the Romans and become the new king of Israel.

So two of the disciples—brothers named James and John—come to Jesus without the others knowing. They ask Jesus to give them special treatment over the other disciples, once he becomes king of Israel. They ask, "When you are sitting on the throne in Jerusalem, can we each sit on your left and right sides?" The two brothers are not asking for actual chairs on either side of Jesus' throne. Instead, they're asking Jesus if they can have the next highest positions of power and authority in Jerusalem—under Jesus, but over everyone else, including the other disciples.

These brothers still do not understand that Jesus is going to Jerusalem to die, not to take over. So, if the two brothers want to have special treatment over the other disciples and be extra close to Jesus, it won't be by sitting next to Jesus on a throne. Jesus says that, if they want to be closer to him than other disciples, they have to be willing to die like him. That is what Jesus means when he asks "Can you drink from this cup and be baptized like me?" Drinking and baptism are figures of speech. Jesus means "Are you willing to suffer and die like me?" They say they are, but they probably still don't understand.

This conversation between Jesus and the brothers is a secret, but the other disciples find out about it and they are angry. They do not like the two brothers taking Jesus to the side and trying to get special treatment.

So, the disciples start to argue. Jesus steps in and stops all of this talk about who has power and authority over whom. In Jesus' kingdom, no one has power and authority over others. Instead, Jesus says that his followers must become servants. That means thinking first of how you can help others, instead of yourself.

That's exactly what Jesus does. Jesus says that even he—the Son of God—came to serve others, not to be served by them. Jesus could have come to earth and taken over the throne in Jerusalem and become a powerful king, with armies and servants. Instead, Jesus came to die so that people could be forgiven of their sins.

James and John want to gain power for themselves, but that is exactly the opposite of what Jesus wants from his followers. Jesus' followers must also be servants to each other, just like Jesus was.

Unit 7

Opposition to Jesus

For the Parent: As anyone who reads the Gospels can see, Jesus' words and actions were met with considerable resistance, particularly by the religious leaders of the day, and to a lesser extent by the political leaders (especially at the end of his life).

But this was to be expected. A noted New Testament scholar puts it this way: if you knew nothing of Christianity and had never heard of Jesus, but you did understand something of the delicate religious and political situation of first-century Palestine, and then you opened up the Gospels and began reading, it would not be long before you stopped and asked, "How long will it take before this Jesus guy gets himself killed?" Jesus' ministry met with considerable opposition because he challenged rigid, blindly traditional understandings of God and the Old Testament as well as the ultimate supremacy of Rome's status as "world power." To the Jewish authorities, Jesus said, "If you know me, you know Yahweh. He sent me." To the Romans he said, "Caesar is OK as far as he goes, but your ultimate allegiance is to the true God, whom I represent."

There is much to be learned about Jesus by paying close attention to his interactions with his opponents. By seeing how Jesus responded to his adversaries, we catch a glimpse from a different angle of how Jesus understood his task on earth. Jesus reveals something of himself in the midst of these debates and struggles.

Lesson 29

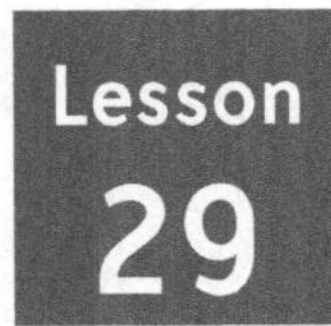

Jesus Upsets a Synagogue Service

What the Parent Should Know: After the story of Jesus' baptism by John (3:1–22) and his temptation in the wilderness (4:1–13), the first story Luke tells of Jesus is one of rejection—in the synagogue of his hometown, by those who knew him best. Such rejection will accompany Jesus throughout his entire life, and it all begins here.

Jesus sweeps into Galilee "in the power of the Spirit" and begins teaching in synagogues throughout the countryside (vv. 14–15). He has already begun to gather a following by the time he gets to his hometown of Nazareth in v. 16 (see especially v. 23). When he arrives at Nazareth, he enters the synagogue, which is his regular practice (v. 16).

It was the custom in the synagogue for someone to read a portion of Scripture and then for one of the men present to instruct others on its meaning. Jesus is handed the scroll of Isaiah and unrolls it to Isaiah 61:1–2. This portion of Isaiah speaks of a coming king, the messiah, who would sit on the throne in Jerusalem and relieve people's burdens: he would bring good news to the poor, give sight to the blind, and release the oppressed. This would finally take place in "the year of the Lord's favor" (v. 19). Here Isaiah is alluding to the Year of Jubilee (Leviticus 25:8–55), prescribed by the Law, when, every fifty years, debts are canceled and slaves set free.

In other words, when the messiah comes, all will be set right and everyone will be able to leave aside past burdens and begin again. Here in his hometown, early in his ministry, Jesus claims that Israel's messianic hope is fulfilled that very day "in your hearing" (v. 21). In other words, Jesus is claiming publicly, for the first time, that he is Israel's king.

The people's immediate reaction is favorable (v. 22)—after all, who would not welcome the coming of the messiah and the relief from burdens? Jesus, however, does not seize the opportunity to amass a popular following. Rather than capitalizing on their initial support, he tells them, "You like me now, but it won't last. You will reject me eventually and I will bring my message to others" (see vv. 23–24). Jesus then illustrates the point in a way that seems calculated to upset his hearers. He recounts two Old Testament stories of two faithful Gentiles, the widow of Zarephath and Naaman the Syrian (vv. 25–27), who more readily accepted the prophets Elijah and Elisha than the Israelites did. In other words, Jesus is saying, "I am your messiah, but you will eventually react to me the same way the Israelites did to Elijah."

Alienating your own hometown at the beginning of your ministry is not the way to make friends and influence people. The men of the synagogue are enraged and take Jesus out to throw him over a hill. But Jesus walks away. This episode announces that rejection by his own people would mark Jesus' ministry, and that Gentiles would also come to know Israel's king.

[Note to Parents: The student lesson focuses on Jesus' rejection, so I have chosen not to add an explanation about the Year of Jubilee. The activity book contains a supplementary explanation and activity on this subject.]

Begin by reading aloud:

Jesus returned to Galilee in the power of the Spirit, and news about him spread through the whole countryside. He taught in their synagogues, and everyone praised him.

He went to Nazareth, where he had been brought up, and on the Sabbath day he went into the synagogue, as was his custom. And he stood up to read. The scroll of the prophet Isaiah was handed to him. Unrolling it, he found the place where it is written:

> "The Spirit of the Lord is on me, because he has anointed me
> to preach good news to the poor.
> He has sent me to proclaim freedom for the prisoners and
> recovery of sight for the blind, to release the oppressed,
> to proclaim the year of the Lord's favor."

Then he rolled up the scroll, gave it back to the attendant, and sat down. The eyes of everyone in the synagogue were fastened on him, and he began by saying to them, "Today this scripture is fulfilled in your hearing."

All spoke well of him and were amazed at the gracious words that came from his lips. "Isn't this Joseph's son?" they asked.

Jesus said to them, "Surely you will quote this proverb to me: 'Physician, heal yourself! Do here in your hometown what we have heard that you did in Capernaum.'"

"I tell you the truth," he continued, "no prophet is accepted in his hometown. I assure you that there were many widows in Israel in

Elijah's time, when the sky was shut for three and a half years and there was a severe famine throughout the land. Yet Elijah was not sent to any of them, but to a widow in Zarephath in the region of Sidon. And there were many in Israel with leprosy in the time of Elisha the prophet, yet not one of them was cleansed—only Naaman the Syrian."

All the people in the synagogue were furious when they heard this. They got up, drove him out of the town, and took him to the brow of the hill on which the town was built, in order to throw him down the cliff. But he walked right through the crowd and went on his way.

This story takes place when Jesus is about thirty years old, near the very beginning of his travels with his disciples. He has been traveling around Galilee, teaching people about God. All of this teaching has made Jesus well known in the region. People like what he has to say, and they praise him for being such a good teacher. But this is about to change! Now, in his own hometown of Nazareth, Jesus will be rejected.

When Jesus arrives in Nazareth, he goes to the synagogue on the Sabbath (the Jewish holy day) to teach. Synagogues were where the Jews gathered to read the Scriptures and pray. The custom back then was for one of the men to read a portion of the Bible and explain it. Bibles were in scrolls back then, not books. A scroll was a long piece of dried animal skin (called parchment) that rolled up like a roll of paper towels. To read from it you had to unroll it and find what you wanted to read.

On this day, Jesus is handed the scroll of the prophet Isaiah. Isaiah was a prophet of Israel who had lived about 700 years before the time of Jesus and wrote one of the books of the Old Testament. Jesus turns to a part of the scroll that talks about the king that is coming to help Israel, and what he will do when he comes. Isaiah's prophecy tells the listeners that the king will rescue the poor and those in prison, give sight to the blind, and help those who are mistreated by powerful people.

When Jesus finishes reading this part of Isaiah, he sits down and then says something astounding: "Today this scripture is fulfilled in your hearing." Jesus is telling them that he is Israel's king! He is the one who will help the poor, the prisoners, the blind, and those who are mistreated by powerful people.

Everyone in the synagogue is delighted to hear this. They have been waiting hundreds of years for their king to come help those in need. Now, finally, he is here. But then Jesus says something that makes them angry with him. He tells them, "You may like me now, but one day you are going to turn your backs on me."

   Lesson 29: Jesus Upsets a Synagogue Service

Jesus explains what he means by using Old Testament stories they all know, the stories of the great prophets Elijah and Elisha. Most Israelites did not listen to Elijah and Elisha, but two Gentiles *did* listen—a widow who lived in Zarephath and a man named Naaman. Jesus is telling the people of his own town that they will one day turn their backs on him just like the Israelites turned their backs on Elijah and Elisha. And just like in the prophets' day, the Gentiles will turn to Jesus and follow him.

The people of Jesus' hometown become absolutely furious when they hear that. They cannot stand the thought that their own king will be accepted by Gentiles. After all, their enemies, the Romans, are Gentiles! The crowd is so angry that they all cluster around Jesus and march him to a cliff to throw him off.

But Jesus is right. His own countrymen should be the first ones to follow Jesus and trust him. But for the rest of his life, many of his own people will oppose him—and many Gentiles will follow Jesus and trust him.

<table>
<tr><td>Lesson
30</td><td>Matthew 16:5–12

False Teaching Spreads like Yeast</td></tr>
</table>

What the Parent Should Know: In this passage, Jesus and his disciples had just left the town of Magadan (also known as Magdala, home of Mary Magdalene), on the Sea of Galilee. There, in an attempt to discredit him, the Pharisees and Sadducees had tested Jesus to see if he could produce a "sign from heaven" (16:1). Jesus completely disarmed his opposition by not even acknowledging the legitimacy of their question (16:2–4).

After this confrontation, Jesus and the disciples cross back over the Sea of Galilee. The twelve disciples have forgotten to bring bread for their meals. Jesus, seizing an everyday moment as an object lesson, warns the disciples to beware of the Pharisees and Sadducees. The harmful influence of these supposed experts of the Law is like yeast in a loaf of bread.

Earlier in Matthew, yeast is a positive influence (13:31–33; see Year One, Lesson 3). Elsewhere, however, yeast is a metaphor for something that is pervasive and has a bad influence (1 Corinthians 5:6–7; Galatians 5:9), which is how Jesus is using the metaphor here. Just as even a little pinch of yeast spreads and causes the entire loaf to rise, the false teaching of the

Pharisees and Sadducees works its way into the hearts and minds of listeners and quickly has a corrupting influence.

Amazingly, the disciples do not have a clue about what Jesus is talking about. Jesus is clearly connecting yeast with the Pharisees and Sadducees, but the disciples think he is talking about their forgetting to bring bread with them (v. 7). In response, Jesus tells them that they have little faith.

This was not a slap on the wrist but a sharp rebuke for their lack of spiritual perception. Why, after Jesus had just fed 4,000 with a few loaves (15:29–39), would the disciples think Jesus was fretting about bread? Not only that, but Jesus has already told them directly that yeast was a metaphor for the Pharisees and Sadducees. Verse 11 is an understatement: "How is it that you don't understand that I was not talking about bread?" In contemporary idiom this might be, "How can you be so dimwitted?"

Jesus is stunned at his disciples' lack of perception, but not because Jesus is an impatient teacher. Rather, Jesus rebukes them because the stakes are so high. What the Pharisees and Sadducees were teaching the people about God was not just wrong or inaccurate in an academic sense. Their teaching was dangerous.

Much of the Sermon on the Mount (Matthew 5–7), explains why this teaching was so dangerous. The leaders added burdens to the law that the law did not require, and so made faith in God an arduous task; they obscured the clear commands of God with their own traditions, and so distorted a true knowledge of God; they were more interested in their own status and power than in serving God and the people, and so stunted the spiritual growth of the very people they were called to lead. Jesus sums this up here and in Matthew 24:13. The religious leaders placed burdens on the people that made them "twice as fit for hell" as they were themselves, a hyperbole meaning twice as unfit for taking part in God's kingdom that Jesus is building.

The false teaching of the religious leaders obscures and distorts a true knowledge of God. Since their teaching spreads so easily, like yeast through a lump of dough, it must be resisted at all costs.

Begin by reading aloud:

When they went across the lake, the disciples forgot to take bread. "Be careful," Jesus said to them. "Be on your guard against the yeast of the Pharisees and Sadducees."

They discussed this among themselves and said, "It is because we didn't bring any bread."

Aware of their discussion, Jesus asked, "You of little faith, why are you talking among yourselves about having no bread? Do you still not

　　　　　　　　　　　　　Lesson 30: False Teaching Spreads like Yeast

understand? Don't you remember the five loaves for the five thousand, and how many basketfuls you gathered? Or the seven loaves for
the four thousand, and how many basketfuls you gathered? How is it
you don't understand that I was not talking to you about bread? But
be on your guard against the yeast of the Pharisees and Sadducees."
Then they understood that he was not telling them to guard against
the yeast used in bread, but against the teaching of the Pharisees
and Sadducees.

In this story, Jesus warns the disciples about the teachings of the
Pharisees and the Sadducees, the religious leaders. Jesus says that what
they teach is sometimes false and dangerous.

What kind of teaching is Jesus objecting to? The leaders are teaching
that the people can make God pleased with them if they follow all sorts
of complicated and strict rules that aren't even in the Bible. Jesus says
that this sort of teaching is dangerous because it leads people away from
knowing God.

Then Jesus gives the disciples a picture of what this false teaching
does. He says the teaching of the Pharisees and Sadducees is like yeast in
a loaf of bread. What does Jesus mean? If you want dough to rise when
you bake bread, you have to add a little yeast. Yeast is a fungus that
mixes together with the dough. Yeast grows very quickly and gives off a
gas called carbon dioxide, which spreads throughout the dough in little
bubbles. When you bake the bread, the bubbles break and leave air pock-
ets in the dough. That is how the dough expands to a loaf that is fluffy
and light. Without yeast you wouldn't have a round loaf of bread but a
flat, heavy bread. But just a tiny pinch of yeast spreads throughout the
whole lump of dough quickly and makes the dough rise.

Yeast is a good thing when you are making bread, but Jesus talks
about yeast to make a point about false teaching. False teaching about
God spreads quickly to a lot of people. Religious leaders are in charge of
teaching the people about God. The people look to them to tell them
what God is like, and they listen to what the leaders say. So, whatever the
leader says spreads right away to everyone who is listening—like yeast in
dough.

Think of a large class of children listening to a teacher talk about
American history. These children are very young and haven't yet learned
very much yet about the presidents. What if the teacher says to the class,
"Abraham Lincoln was the first president"? You know that is not true.
George Washington was the first president. But the children in this class

don't know any better. So they will all leave the class thinking that Abraham Lincoln was the first president.

All it takes is for one teacher to say something wrong and right away the whole class believes it. Now, if you were in that class and heard a teacher talk like this, you would probably say, "Wow, that teacher is completely wrong," and you wouldn't listen to what she said. You know the truth and so you won't be fooled. Jesus is telling the disciples not to be fooled by what the false teachers say. They should listen to Jesus instead. He is the true teacher.

False teaching spreads quickly. And when teachers spread false ideas about God, the listeners won't learn what God is really like. That is why Jesus tells his disciples to be careful about what the leaders are saying. They must listen to Jesus instead.

<table>
<tr><td>Lesson
31</td><td>Matthew 15:1–20
A Clean Heart is Better
than Clean Food</td></tr>
</table>

What the Parent Should Know: This passage is a debate between Jesus and the Pharisees and teachers of the Law over a point of Jewish tradition—the dietary laws. Jesus claims that his teaching takes precedence over any such tradition, even if that tradition is rooted in the Old Testament itself.

Jesus had just walked on the water and crossed over the Sea of Galilee with his disciples to Gennesaret (14:22–36). In their continued effort to discredit Jesus, the Pharisees and teachers of the law accused the disciples of failing to keep "the tradition of the elders" (15:2). "Traditions" developed in Judaism because the Old Testament laws pertaining to ritual requirements are not always perfectly clear on what is required in specific situations. Traditions developed to help clarify what should and should not be done. These traditions began orally and were eventually written down and became the Mishnah around AD 200. (The Mishnah kept expanding, and became known as the Talmud around AD 500).

In this passage, the specific tradition in view is the washing of hands before eating. The concern is not bacteria and disease but ritual cleanliness. The law commands Jews to eat only food that is considered ritually clean

(Leviticus 11:1–23; Deuteronomy 14:3–21). This is one of the ways that the Israelites maintain their distinctiveness among the other nations. To be unclean is a serious concern, for uncleanness brings one to a symbolic state of disharmony with God and fellow Israelites. Ritual hand washing is a tradition that developed as an extra measure to make sure nothing unclean would accidentally enter someone's mouth. Apparently neither Jesus nor his disciples maintain this tradition, which gives Jesus' opponents an opportunity to discredit them—and him—for not having religious fervor.

Jesus turns the tables on his accusers by exposing their hypocrisy. Sure, the religious leaders keep their traditions, but they think nothing of breaking God's clear commands in Scripture. The example Jesus gives concerns the fifth commandment, "Honor your mother and father" (v. 4; see Exodus 20:12; 21:17; Deuteronomy 5:16; Leviticus 20:9). The Pharisees taught that the monetary help one could give to one's parents could be given instead to the temple as a "gift devoted to God," safely tucked away in the temple treasury (see also Mark 7:9–13 for more details). Thus, Jesus argues, the tradition nullifies the intention of the command. The tradition, as Isaiah 29:13 says (vv. 8–9), pays lip service to God while neglecting what God actually commands.

After rebuking the Pharisees, Jesus turns to the crowd and begins teaching them (which greatly offends the Pharisees, since Jesus is in essence relieving these "blind guides" of their teaching role). Jesus teaches the crowd a new way of thinking about what is clean and what is unclean. True cleanliness is not a matter of ritual hand washing. In fact, it is not even about what you eat. True cleanliness is a matter of what comes out of a person, not what goes in (vv. 10–12).

By redefining clean and unclean, Jesus declares not only the traditions to be passé, but the Old Testament purity laws themselves. (Mark is very clear on this when he explains that Jesus declares all foods clean in contrast to the Old Testament; Mark 7:19; see also Acts 10:9–23.) Cleanliness and uncleanliness are no longer matters of ritual observance but of the heart and mind translated into action (vv. 19–20). "Clean" and "unclean" are no longer passive notions of what outside elements can do to you. Cleanliness is now an active matter of what you consciously do and say.

For the religious leaders of Jesus' day, whose job it was to protect ancient tradition, Jesus' announcement constitutes open rebellion. But the kingdom of heaven is not about maintaining rituals, but rather creating in its citizens a clean heart that translates into a godly life.

Begin by reading aloud:

Then some Pharisees and teachers of the law came to Jesus from Jerusalem and asked, "Why do your disciples break the tradition of the
elders? They don't wash their hands before they eat!"

Jesus replied, "And why do you break the command of God for
the sake of your tradition? For God said, 'Honor your father and
mother' and 'Anyone who curses his father or mother must be put to
death.' But you say that if a man says to his father or mother, 'Whatever help you might otherwise have received from me is a gift devoted
to God,' he is not to 'honor his father' with it. Thus you nullify the
word of God for the sake of your tradition. You hypocrites! Isaiah was
right when he prophesied about you:

> " 'These people honor me with their lips, but their hearts are
> far from me. They worship me in vain; their teachings are but
> rules taught by men.' "

Jesus called the crowd to him and said, "Listen and understand.
What goes into a man's mouth does not make him 'unclean,' but what
comes out of his mouth, that is what makes him 'unclean.' "

Then the disciples came to him and asked, "Do you know that the
Pharisees were offended when they heard this?"

He replied, "Every plant that my heavenly Father has not planted
will be pulled up by the roots. Leave them; they are blind guides. If a
blind man leads a blind man, both will fall into a pit."

Peter said, "Explain the parable to us."

"Are you still so dull?" Jesus asked them. "Don't you see that
whatever enters the mouth goes into the stomach and then out of
the body? But the things that come out of the mouth come from the
heart, and these make a man 'unclean.' For out of the heart come
evil thoughts, murder, adultery, sexual immorality, theft, false testimony, slander. These are what make a man 'unclean'; but eating with
unwashed hands does not make him 'unclean.' "

In this story, Jesus is teaching the people that a clean heart is more
important to God than the kind of food you eat. That may seem strange
for us to hear, but this was a big issue in Jesus' day.

Some of the laws in the Old Testament talk about the kinds of foods
the Israelites could eat and not eat. Foods they were allowed to eat, like
fruit, lamb, and vegetables, were called "clean." Foods that were not
allowed, like pork, were called "unclean." Clean and unclean had nothing

     Lesson 31: A Clean Heart is Better than Clean Food

to do with dirt or bacteria. In the Old Testament, God told the Israelites to keep away from certain foods to show that the Israelites were different from the people around them.

Eating unclean food was a big deal for the Israelites, because whoever ate unclean food was unclean, too. If someone was unclean, he was not allowed to worship God or be near other Israelites—that is what the Old Testament law says. He had to be off by himself for a while, usually for a few days, until the priests said it was OK to come back.

To make extra sure that people did not eat unclean food by mistake, the teachers of the law came up with an idea—everybody had to wash their hands before they ate anything. This was a "tradition of the elders." It wasn't part of the Old Testament—it was an additional rule meant to keep people from accidentally breaking part of the Old Testament law.

This would be like your mother, who is going out shopping, telling you not to eat the cake in the refrigerator. After she leaves, your older brother says, "Just to be safe, don't even open the refrigerator at all, or else you might forget yourself and take a cake."

In this story some Pharisees and teachers of the law accuse Jesus' disciples of disobeying the "traditions of the elders." These traditions were hundreds of years old. The leaders taught that if you broke one of these rules, God would be angry with you. They want to make Jesus and his disciples look like they don't care what God thinks of them, so they say, "You don't follow these rules!"

Jesus tells the Pharisees and the teachers of the law that being clean or unclean doesn't have anything to do with food. Instead, Jesus teaches that what makes people clean or unclean isn't the food that goes into their stomach. After all, whatever you eat comes out when you go to the bathroom!

What makes us clean is what's in our heart—the kinds of thoughts we have inside of us, the way we feel towards others, and the decisions we make. Jesus says that the kinds of thoughts we have usually wind up becoming the things we do. If you are jealous of your brother, sooner or later you will do something unkind to him. If you are angry with a friend because she was mean to you, sooner or later you will lose your temper with her—or maybe even hit her.

Jesus is teaching that God cares about your thoughts are and what you do to others. Those are the things that make us clean or unclean, not food.

What the Parent Should Know: In this passage, Jesus for the first time in Matthew's Gospel explains to his disciples what must happen to him in Jerusalem—suffering at the hands of the religious leaders, death, and resurrection. By now the disciples should be prepared for this news. Peter's confession that Jesus is "the Christ, the Son of the living God" just several verses earlier (Matthew 16:16, Lesson 25) suggested that, maybe, they had finally begun to see the big picture. But Peter is not willing to allow Jesus to accept his own death sentence so casually, so he takes Jesus aside and tells him so: "Never, Lord! . . . This shall never happen to you!" Jesus, however, teaches the disciples that denial of self is not only his goal but also the pattern of living for the disciples.

Jesus was not the first would-be messiah Judea had ever seen. Others had taken up the mantle of Jewish liberator from Rome, and these messiahs often met with early and violent death. Clearly, Peter at least still has some expectation that Jesus is a messiah of the same mold. The last thing Peter or the disciples want is for Jesus to head up another crash-and-burn revolutionary movement—and this cause is best served by keeping Jesus alive, not sending him to certain death.

Jesus rebukes Peter in the strongest of terms for unwittingly opposing the very purpose of his mission: he calls Peter Satan (v. 23). At the beginning of Jesus' ministry (Year One, Lesson 29, Matthew 4:1–11), Satan unsuccessfully tempted Jesus in the wilderness from carrying out the Father's mission. Now, as Jesus is nearing the end of his ministry, Jesus sees in Peter's rebuke another Satan-like attempt to thwart the divine plan of suffering, death, and resurrection. Of course, Jesus is not saying that Peter "is" Satan, or even that Peter is a mouthpiece for Satan. Note that in v. 23, Jesus says that Peter has in mind the "things of men." Rather, Jesus calls Peter Satan because he recognizes in Peter's words the same fundamental temptation to accept some earthly kingdom (4:8–9), and thus veer away from God's course.

Jesus continues by telling the disciples that following him means choosing the very same path of suffering and self-denial (vv. 24–26). For Christians who are subject to political persecution, "losing one's life" often means literal death. All Christians, however, are faced with the same challenge of losing one's life in another sense: daily surrender to God to seek his ways, not one's own. And just as Peter opposed Jesus in fulfilling his mission, Christians too often oppose Jesus when it comes to laying down their own lives—their own comforts and private agendas.

In the same way that Jesus' goal is not a throne in Jerusalem, power, or gaining wealth, but suffering and loss of life, following Jesus means living a life of self-denial. The benefit is that you gain your soul rather than the world. By this Jesus means that a life of self-denial begins to shape one's whole being so that it conforms more and more to God's plan for us rather than what we or others might aspire to. Self-denial is the Christian way of living, the very thing Jesus himself modeled explicitly.

[Note to Parents: The passage includes vv. 27 and 28, which raise two issues that are perplexing enough for adults (and biblical scholars), let alone young children. The first (v. 27) speaks of rewards given out by God for one's behavior, which to young ears can sound like needing to earn God's favor. The second (v. 28) seems to say that Jesus would return before some of his disciples met their death. There are various interpretations commentators give to these widely contested verses, and each one takes more maturity than a young child can be expected to possess.]

Begin by reading aloud:

> From that time on Jesus began to explain to his disciples that he must go to Jerusalem and suffer many things at the hands of the elders, chief priests, and teachers of the law, and that he must be killed and on the third day be raised to life.
>
> Peter took him aside and began to rebuke him. "Never, Lord!" he said. "This shall never happen to you!"
>
> Jesus turned and said to Peter, "Get behind me, Satan! You are a stumbling block to me; you do not have in mind the things of God, but the things of men."
>
> Then Jesus said to his disciples, "If anyone would come after me, he must deny himself and take up his cross and follow me. For whoever wants to save his life will lose it, but whoever loses his life for me will find it. What good will it be for a man if he gains the whole world, yet forfeits his soul? Or what can a man give in exchange for his soul?"

In this story, Jesus is teaching his disciples a lesson about how they should live their lives every day. Following Jesus means that our thoughts should be on serving God and serving each other, and not on thinking of ourselves first. Jesus calls that kind of living "losing your life." Living this way brings us closer to God.

Jesus begins by telling his disciples that he is going to suffer and die when they get to Jerusalem, and then after three days he will rise from the dead. He has tried telling the disciples this before, but they did not understand. Now, Jesus wants to make sure the disciples understand exactly what will happen to him before they get to Jerusalem.

When Peter hears this from Jesus, he says, "No way, Jesus. We're not going to let that happen to you!" Peter and the disciples are shocked to hear Jesus say he has to die. They are counting on Jesus to be a normal earthly king. They want Jesus to march into Jerusalem and defeat the Romans with an army. They do not want Jesus to die on a cross. What kind of a king would he be if he went to his capital city and immediately was put to death?

Peter thinks he is helping Jesus by saying, "We won't let you die, Jesus." But Peter is not helping. Peter does not understand that Jesus <u>has</u> to suffer and die for our sins. Peter means well, but he is getting in Jesus' way. That is why Jesus calls Peter "Satan" and tells him to get out of the way. Of course, Jesus does not mean that Peter is Satan. That is a figure of speech. Jesus just means that what Peter wants is the exact opposite of what God and Jesus want.

But Jesus is talking about more than his own suffering and dying. Jesus says that his followers will have to "die" too. He says they will have to take up their cross and lose their lives. It sounds like Jesus is saying, "You will all die like I am going to die—suffering on a cross." But Jesus does not mean that. He is using a figure of speech. He is telling the disciples to spend their lives serving God and serving others, rather than thinking about themselves first.

Living like that can be hard, and Jesus knows it. But this is how he wants us to live every day. Jesus lived that way, too. He served God and others everywhere he went. He even died on the cross for our sins. Jesus is selfless, and he wants all who follow him to have the same selfless attitude.

   Lesson 32: Surrendering our Lives to God Every Day

Unit 8

The End of Jesus' Life

For the Parent: The four Gospels all have different emphases and nuances, but one area where there is considerable overlap is the account of the Passion Week, the last week of Jesus' life.

Although the focus of the Passion Week accounts is certainly on Jesus' death and resurrection, there are numerous other events of the week that contribute to the overall portrait of Jesus that is being painted: his entry to Jerusalem, which caused a stir for all sorts of reasons; Jesus' move to confront the religious leaders rather than align with them; the circumstances surrounding his trial; the true tragedy of his death and triumph of his resurrection. The events of this week show the final purpose of Jesus' life and are a bridge to the remaining books of the New Testament.

The purpose of this unit is not to cover the entire story of Jesus' death and resurrection, but rather to begin to study some parts of it in depth. The later years of this curriculum will return to this story again and again to complete the student's understanding.

The assumption is that the student will have already heard the full story in other contexts. However, if you wish to add to this unit, you may read selections from Matthew 27–28, Mark 15–16, Luke 23–24, or John 19–20.

Obey God More than Caesar

What the Parent Should Know: During the Passion Week, tensions are running high between Jesus and the Jewish leaders. That is hardly a surprise since Jesus begins the week by turning over the tables of the moneychangers in the temple (21:12–17) and generally condemning the Pharisees (see the exchanges in Matthew 21–23). At first, the Pharisees go head to head with Jesus—trying to assert their authority over him. But now they change tactics by bringing the Roman government into the picture. They are trying to trap Jesus into committing the arrestable offense of treason against Caesar. As usual, Jesus turns the tables, outwits his accusers, and seizes the opportunity to spiritually challenge his listeners.

You should know that, as this story begins, the Pharisees have formed an unexpected alliance with the Herodians. The Pharisees were strongly opposed to Roman rule, while the Herodians were a political party that supported the rule of the Herods. (The Herodian Dynasty began when the Edomites were conquered by the Jewish ruler John Hyrcanus in the late second century BC and forced to convert to Judaism. A complex series of events followed, with Herod the Great establishing his authority over all of Judea in 37 BC. The dynasty owed its continued status to the Romans and so were submissive to them, whereas the Pharisees longed for liberation.)

Together, the two groups plan to trap Jesus into committing a political crime: advocating that the people under Herod's rule should not pay taxes to the current Caesar (Tiberius), as the law requires.

They approach Jesus with false flattery. They call him "Teacher" and praise him for his integrity in paying no respect to status (v. 16). Of course, this is anything but praiseworthy to them. Quite the opposite: they find it infuriating that Jesus persistently undermines their authority. Having flattered him—and hopefully brought his defenses down—they ask Jesus whether he thinks people should pay taxes to Caesar. They are banking on Jesus being forthright, as he typically is, which would result in his committing an obvious act of insurrection. They presume that Jesus is just like every other "messiah" of the time: looking for a way to rid the Jews of their Roman overlords. The Pharisees are hoping to play on Jesus' political ambition.

Jesus handles this situation not only with his characteristic cleverness, but with a theological lesson. He shows them a coin—a denarius, about a day's wage. Caesar's picture was on one side, and an inscription on the other: "Tiberius Caesar Augustus, son of the divine Augustus." Since Caesar's picture and inscription are stamped onto the coin, it shows that the coin is rightfully his. So, Jesus is basically saying, "This coin belongs to Caesar, so let him have it." Challenging Caesar's secular authority is not on Jesus' mind at all. The attempt to trap Jesus has failed.

Jesus, however, issues a counter-challenge to the Pharisees that seems simple enough but is loaded with theological depth: "Give to Caesar what is Caesar's but give to God what is God's" (v. 21). This means more than just "pay taxes to Caesar but give your heart to God." Caesar was worshiped as a god, and Jesus' remark is a swipe at that belief. Jesus is saying that Caesar has his limited realm of authority, but God rules over all, including Caesar. Allegiance to Caesar means paying him his taxes, but allegiance to God means worshiping him alone as God, not the false god Caesar.

The coin has a deeper meaning as an object lesson for Jesus' identity. The coin has Caesar's image and inscription on it—everyone who looks at the coin knows it belongs to Caesar and that they need to obey him. Jesus is like a coin. Jesus bears God's image, so to speak, as the coin bears the image of Caesar—as we read elsewhere, Jesus is the "image of the invisible God" (Colossians 1:15), the "exact representation" of God's being (Hebrews 1:3). Jesus is saying, "When you look at the coin, you see Caesar. Do what Caesar says. When you look at me, you see God. Do what God says—which is what I say."

Jesus is neither interested in replacing Caesar on his throne, nor is he so naïve as to be manipulated into the Pharisees' trap. His focus remains on calling people to a deeper knowledge of God.

Begin by reading aloud:

> Then the Pharisees went out and laid plans to trap him in his words. They sent their disciples to him along with the Herodians. "Teacher," they said, "we know you are a man of integrity and that you teach the way of God in accordance with the truth. You aren't swayed by men, because you pay no attention to who they are. Tell us then, what is your opinion? Is it right to pay taxes to Caesar or not?"
>
> But Jesus, knowing their evil intent, said, "You hypocrites, why are you trying to trap me? Show me the coin used for paying the tax." They brought him a denarius, and he asked them, "Whose portrait is this? And whose inscription?"
>
> "Caesar's," they replied.

Then he said to them, "Give to Caesar what is Caesar's, and to God what is God's."

When they heard this, they were amazed. So they left him and went away.

This story occurs during the week before Jesus is crucified. The religious leaders, especially the Pharisees, have been angry with Jesus for years because Jesus has been telling the people to listen to him instead of them. Now they are going to try to trap Jesus into breaking the law so he can be arrested.

The Pharisees are so determined to get rid of Jesus that they even team up with their enemies, a group of people called "Herodians." The Herodians support the rule of kings who come from the Herod family—and the Herod family is in power because the Romans put them there. So the Herodians like the Romans being in power over the Jews.

The Pharisees do not! They want the Herod family *and* Romans gone from their land. Pharisees and Herodians do not get along, but both of them want Jesus gone. So they decide to work together to find a way to get Jesus arrested.

They try to trap Jesus by asking him whether he thinks people should obey the Roman law and pay taxes to the Roman emperor, Tiberius Caesar. They hope that Jesus will say "no" so they can have him arrested by the Romans.

Not paying your taxes was a serious crime back then. Today if you don't pay your taxes, you might have to pay a fine. If you don't pay taxes for a long time, you might eventually spend some time in jail. But in Jesus' day, some Jews did not want to pay taxes because they thought it was wrong that the Romans were ruling over them. Not paying taxes was treason: rebellion against the king. If you didn't pay your taxes, you could be arrested and put to death.

But Jesus doesn't allow himself to be tricked by the Pharisees. He tells the Pharisees to take out a coin and look at it. This coin was called a denarius, and it was about what a person would earn for doing one day's work. Like our coins today, there was a picture on one side and a saying on the other. The picture on the coin was of Caesar. On the other side was a saying, "Tiberius Caesar Augustus, son of the divine Augustus." Augustus was Tiberius's stepfather and Augustus was worshipped by the Romans as a god. So, this coin said to anyone who held it, "This coin belongs to Tiberius, the son of the god Augustus" (which made Tiberius a god, too).

Jesus doesn't care about coins and taxes. Remember, his kingdom is the kingdom of heaven, where people learn to love God and follow him. Jesus' kingdom is not a kingdom of palaces, armies, and taxes. So Jesus says, "This is Caesar's coin. If he wants it, give it to him."

But that is not all Jesus has to say. He doesn't just tell them to give to Caesar what belongs to Caesar. Jesus tells them they also have to give to God what belongs to God. That means, "Pay taxes to Caesar. But Caesar is not god. The real God is the one I am teaching you about. Listen to what I tell you about God."

Think of it this way. The coin has Caesar's picture on one side. Everyone who looks at the coin knows it belongs to Caesar and that they need to obey Caesar by paying taxes. In a way, Jesus is like a coin, too. Everyone who looks at Jesus and hears what he says needs to worship God. Jesus is saying, "When you look at the coin, you see Caesar. Do what Caesar says and pay taxes. When you look at me, you see God. Do what God says and worship only him, not Caesar."

<table>
<tr><td>Lesson
34</td><td>Matthew 26:17–28

Jesus Introduces a New Exodus</td></tr>
</table>

What the Parent Should Know: On the eve of his crucifixion, Jesus celebrates with his disciples the Passover meal—Israel's ancient commemoration of its deliverance from Egyptian slavery. On this particular night, however, the symbolism of Israel's deliverance takes on new meaning. From now on, it will commemorate Jesus' sacrificial death on the cross.

The Passover meal was a yearly celebration of Israel's deliverance, a reminder to each passing generation of God's act of mercy to his people (Exodus 12:24–28; 13:14–16). The "destroyer" (Exodus 12:23) went through Egypt and killed the firstborn of every house, but "passed over" those houses that had the blood of the Passover lamb on the doorframes. The Passover meal included unleavened bread (matzah), which marked Israel's rapid departure from Egypt (as there was no time to bake the bread properly), bitter herbs symbolizing Israel's bitter enslavement, and an unblemished lamb (Exodus 12:1–11).

While partaking of this meal, Jesus refers to the bread as "my body" (v. 26) and the wine as "my blood of the covenant" (v. 28). The elements that symbolized the deliverance of Hebrew slaves now symbolize Jesus' death. As the Israelites were delivered from the slavery of Egypt, so now all men and women can be delivered from the slavery of sin. The broken bread of the meal now symbolizes Jesus' own soon-to-be broken body. The blood of the lamb that delivered the Israelites from the "destroyer" now symbolizes Jesus' own blood that will deliver his people from sin and death.

The Exodus as a whole is also given a new meaning. The Exodus was the event that formed the Israelites into a nation, the event that, properly speaking, marks Israel's beginning. (Before the Exodus, Israel was not a nation but a large family tribe that had its beginnings with Abraham. When Israel left Egypt, it began to function more like a nation.)

In the same way, Jesus' death and resurrection mark the beginning of a new people of God—not a nation marked by ethnic identity, but a people made up of all those who believe, Jew and Gentile, united as one people in their faith in Christ (Galatians 3:26–29). That kind of deliverance requires a sacrifice much more costly than an unblemished lamb. It requires the sacrifice of God's Son, "a lamb without blemish or defect" (1 Peter 1:19).

Amid this sober celebration, Jesus also predicts that Judas will betray him. Jesus explains to the disciples that the betrayal is necessary, though it is still a woeful act on Judas' part (v. 24). Judas vehemently denies Jesus' charge (v. 25), but this only paints him in a more sinister light. In the ancient world, as in the modern Middle East, to eat with someone at the table is a sign of trust. By sitting down with Jesus and lying to his face, Judas is blatantly betraying that trust—he is a traitor. Yet, it is Judas' betrayal that allows the symbolism of the Lord's Supper to become a reality. The bread is about to be broken; the lamb is about to be slain. A new Exodus is about to occur.

[Note to Parents: This lesson ends at v. 28. Verse 29 is a cryptic statement about the future that is puzzling enough for adults. It is best to focus on the symbolism of the Last Supper and Judas' betrayal rather than address Jesus' cryptic comment about the future.]

Begin by reading aloud:

> On the first day of the Feast of Unleavened Bread, the disciples came to Jesus and asked, "Where do you want us to make preparations for you to eat the Passover?"
>
> He replied, "Go into the city to a certain man and tell him, 'The Teacher says: My appointed time is near. I am going to celebrate the

   Lesson 34: Jesus Introduces a New Exodus

Passover with my disciples at your house.'" So the disciples did as Jesus had directed them and prepared the Passover.

When evening came, Jesus was reclining at the table with the Twelve. And while they were eating, he said, "I tell you the truth, one of you will betray me."

They were very sad and began to say to him one after the other, "Surely not I, Lord?"

Jesus replied, "The one who has dipped his hand into the bowl with me will betray me. The Son of Man will go just as it is written about him. But woe to that man who betrays the Son of Man! It would be better for him if he had not been born."

Then Judas, the one who would betray him, said, "Surely not I, Rabbi?"

Jesus answered, "Yes, it is you."

While they were eating, Jesus took bread, gave thanks, and broke it, and gave it to his disciples, saying, "Take and eat; this is my body."

Then he took the cup, gave thanks, and offered it to them, saying, "Drink from it, all of you. This is my blood of the covenant, which is poured out for many for the forgiveness of sins."

In this story, Jesus is eating a meal with his disciples. Before you can understand what Jesus is doing, you need to know about the Feast of Unleavened Bread—the Passover. The Passover was a celebration of one of the greatest events in Israel's history.

In the Old Testament, the Israelites were slaves in Egypt for hundreds of years until God delivered them. On the night before they left Egypt, God told the Israelites that the oldest child of every house would die, because Pharaoh (the king of Egypt) had refused again and again to let the Israelites go. The Israelites were told to put some blood from a sacrificed lamb over the doors of the houses. The blood on the doors of the houses would protect the Israelites—death would "pass over" the houses and the Israelites would be safe. That is why the Israelites called this feast the Passover.

Right before they left Egypt, the Israelites ate a meal. Part of that meal was unleavened bread—bread made without yeast. Yeast is a fungus that makes bread dough rise up into a big round loaf shape, but it takes time to let the dough rise. When the Israelites left Egypt, they were in a hurry so God told them to eat unleavened bread—which is flat and tasteless, but can be made quickly. Along with the unleavened bread, the Israelites also ate the sacrificed lamb at the Passover meal.

Each year after that, the Israelites remember their deliverance from Egypt by celebrating the Passover meal. The Passover meal is the meal Jesus and his disciples are having in this story. It is Thursday evening, the day before Good Friday when Jesus will be crucified.

Even though this is the Passover meal, this time is different than any other time before. Jesus takes the unleavened bread, breaks a piece off, and passes it on to the next person. Jesus says of the bread, "This is my body." Jesus means that his body will be broken on the cross, just like the bread was broken at the meal.

Next Jesus takes the cup of wine and says, "This is my blood." Jesus means that he is going to be put to death and his blood will save the people, like the lamb's blood saved the Israelites from death.

In churches today, we celebrate the same meal Jesus had with his disciples. We usually call it the Lord's Supper or sometimes Communion or Eucharist (which means thanksgiving). Whenever you celebrate the Lord's Supper in church, you are remembering that Jesus died on the cross to forgive sins.

Something else has already happened in this story, though. When they all sat down, before they ate anything, Jesus told the disciples something that surprised and shocked them. "One of you will betray me," Jesus said. They all said, "No way, not *me*!" Even Judas said that, but he was lying. And Jesus knew it. He said, "Yes, it is you, Judas."

Jesus knew that Judas would betray him and that he would be handed over to the Romans and the religious leaders to be nailed to a cross. This is not a surprise to Jesus. It is the purpose of his mission on earth. And that is what he tells the disciples during the Passover meal. "My body will be broken, just like the bread. And my blood will save the people, just like the blood of the lamb. I will forgive their sins."

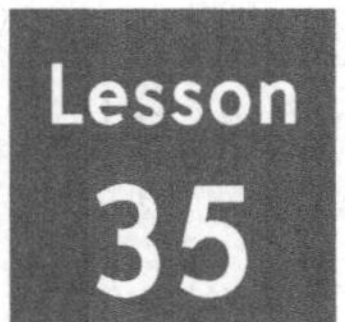

Matthew 26:36–46

Jesus Suffers and Prays Alone

What the Parent Should Know: After the Last Supper, Jesus and his disciples went to Gethsemane, which is on the Mount of Olives near Jerusalem (Gethsemane means "oil press" and John 18:1 and 26 refer to it as a garden).

According to Luke 22:39, Jesus was accustomed to going to the Mount of Olives to pray. Now, a short time before his arrest, Jesus was going there one last time to pray, this time for the strength to go through his horrible ordeal.

When they arrived at Gethsemane, Jesus parted company with most of the disciples and took only Peter and the sons of Zebedee (James and John) with him. Why only three and why these three specifically is something Matthew does not explain. Mark, however, has the same three accompany Jesus when he raised Jairus's daughter from the dead (5:37). Perhaps these three were closer confidants to Jesus than the other nine. (And this may help shed some light on the tensions among the disciples in Mark 10:35–45 [Lesson 28] when James and John ask Jesus about sitting on his left and right side in glory. See also the tensions in Matthew 18:1–4 [Lesson 26].)

Jesus was in agony in Gethsemane. We read that Jesus was "sorrowful and troubled" and "overwhelmed with sorrow to the point of death" (vv. 37–38), and when he went off alone to pray, he "fell with his face to the ground" (v. 39). Today we might say that someone acting like this is incapacitated with fear and sadness. This is not a tough, stoic Jesus, gritting his teeth and pushing through. The thought of enduring what he knew was before him was a heavy burden that Jesus did not want to bear; he was pleading for some way to be relieved of his duty. And so he asked the Father to take the cup from him (v. 39). Drinking a cup is a metaphor for suffering that must be endured (20:22–24; Psalm 11:6). The cup is also an Old Testament metaphor for God's wrath (Isaiah 51:17; see also Lesson 28). Both senses seem to be at work here: the suffering Jesus must endure is the cup of God's wrath. Jesus the innocent will drink the cup on behalf of the guilty.

When Jesus finished praying the first time, he returned to Peter, James, and John and found them sleeping. Jesus asked them why they were not able to "keep watch" with him even for an hour (v. 40). Jesus addressed Peter in particular, since he will be the one to deny Jesus later that evening (vv. 31–35 and 69–75). Jesus went back to pray and this scene is repeated two more times. There are many details of Jesus' life that are not recorded. So why emphasize this scene of Jesus' prayer and his disciples' weakness?

The purpose is not to embarrass the disciples. Rather, the scene highlights how alone Jesus was in his personal agony. Even Jesus' closest friends cannot relate to what Jesus is up against, however well-intentioned they may be. Jesus' task is wholly outside of their realm of experience. The burden Jesus must bear is his alone. He will have no help. In fact, in the next chapter, even God himself will abandon him (Matthew 27:46).

Nevertheless, entirely alone and wishing that he could find some way of getting out of his suffering, Jesus surrenders to the will of the Father.

Begin by reading aloud:

Then Jesus went with his disciples to a place called Gethsemane, and he said to them, "Sit here while I go over there and pray." He took Peter and the two sons of Zebedee along with him, and he began to be sorrowful and troubled. Then he said to them, "My soul is overwhelmed with sorrow to the point of death. Stay here and keep watch with me."

Going a little farther, he fell with his face to the ground and prayed, "My Father, if it is possible, may this cup be taken from me. Yet not as I will, but as you will."

Then he returned to his disciples and found them sleeping. "Could you men not keep watch with me for one hour?" he asked Peter. "Watch and pray so that you will not fall into temptation. The spirit is willing, but the body is weak."

He went away a second time and prayed, "My Father, if it is not possible for this cup to be taken away unless I drink it, may your will be done."

When he came back, he again found them sleeping, because their eyes were heavy. So he left them and went away once more and prayed the third time, saying the same thing.

Then he returned to the disciples and said to them, "Are you still sleeping and resting? Look, the hour is near, and the Son of Man is betrayed into the hands of sinners. Rise, let us go! Here comes my betrayer!"

After Jesus and the disciples eat the Passover meal, they go to the Mount of Olives. These are hills just outside of the city of Jerusalem. In these hills is a place called Gethsemane. That word means "oil press." (Olive oil was used in Jesus' day for things like food and lamp oil.)

Jesus liked going to the Mount of Olives to pray. This night, Jesus knows that he is going to be arrested, tortured, and then hung on a cross to die. Jesus is greatly troubled about this. He knows how difficult it will be to suffer and die. So, Jesus goes to pray to God because he wants to know if God really wants him to go through with it. Jesus takes with him three of his closest disciples to keep him company, Peter, James, and John, but soon Jesus will be left all alone.

Jesus first prays, "Let this cup pass from me." "Cup" is a figure of speech. In the Old Testament it means "suffering." So, drinking the cup means going through suffering. Jesus is asking God if there is some way for him to do God's will without suffering, without "drinking the cup."

Jesus is not telling God he refuses to go through the suffering. He asks God if there is some way he can get out of it, because Jesus is distressed at the thought of suffering and dying. But, Jesus also tells God that he will do what God wants.

All of us sometimes have to do something that makes us nervous, and can even scare us, but we know we have to do it anyway. If you have ever had to go to the hospital for an operation, you might have been up all of the night before worrying about it. You know that once you get there, you will have to leave your parents in the waiting room and be wheeled into the operating room. There you have to be all by yourself, in a strange room with doctors and nurses around you wearing masks, without your family to comfort you. But even though you just want to go home, you go through with it anyway because your parents know you need to and you trust your parents.

When Jesus goes to pray, he asks Peter, James, and John to wait for him. Jesus is distressed and wants the company of his friends. But when Jesus comes back they are asleep. This happens three times. The disciples are not lazy. They just don't understand exactly how distressed Jesus is—or what a horrible death he is facing. They're tired, so they just fall asleep waiting for him.

Jesus' heart is heavy and he is anxious about suffering and dying. He wants his closest friends to be with him, but they do not understand. They fall asleep and so Jesus is completely alone.

In a little while, Jesus will be arrested and taken away to be killed. Jesus will be alone again, but he is willing to face his suffering and death. Jesus does not look to get out of it. He surrenders to his Father's will.

<table>
<tr><td>Lesson
36</td><td align="right">Matthew 26:47–56
Jesus Doesn't Fight Back
When Arrested</td></tr>
</table>

What the Parent Should Know: After Jesus finishes praying in Gethsemane, Judas arrives with a large crowd incited by the religious leaders. The crowd, carrying swords and clubs, thinks they need to take this rebel messiah by force. Like so many others, they still believe that Jesus has come to be a political savior. But Jesus, far from resisting arrest, goes willingly, for he is doing the Father's will.

When the crowd arrives, Judas goes to Jesus, calls him Rabbi, and kisses him. These pre-arranged signals reveal Jesus' identity to the crowd. A kiss was not necessarily a sign of affection as in our culture (although it could include that). It was a normal greeting that would not raise any suspicion. Likewise, Judas refers to Jesus as Rabbi ("my teacher"), which is what the disciples normally called Jesus. In today's world Judas might have said, "The one whose hand I shake and call 'sir' is the one to arrest." Jesus responds by calling Judas "Friend," which is not sarcastic but genuine. Jesus was addressing a man who has been part of his inner group for three years. We might even conclude that there is regret and sadness on Jesus' part that his friend has betrayed him like this.

When the crowd grabs Jesus to take him away, one of the three disciples (see v. 37; only John 18:10 identifies him as Peter) cuts off the ear of the servant of the high priest. This disciple, confronted by the arrest of his leader, is reacting naturally—but by now Jesus' message should be clear. Jesus' kingdom is not about swords but inner transformation by the power of God. That is what Jesus means in v. 52, "All who draw the sword will die by the sword." This is a reminder that Jesus' kingdom is not what the disciples have been expecting. Even when he is arrested by a mob with only death in their eyes, Jesus' message remains the same.

Further, Jesus tells this zealous disciple that escape would be an easy task for him. God could send down twelve legions of angels (a legion equals 6,000 men, so 72,000) if he wished. But, had the three stayed awake in Gethsemane, they would have known that Jesus had already addressed all of this with God. Jesus had decided to willingly face suffering and death, as the Father wanted.

Before being taken away, though, Jesus turns to the crowd and dresses them down. They had seen him all the time in public. They could have seen that he was not leading any sort of rebellion. Yet they have waited until now to arrest him in secret.

But even that cowardly act plays its part in the unfolding of the biblical drama, or as Jesus puts it, the fulfillment of Scripture (v. 56). It is unlikely that Jesus has any particular verse or verses of the Old Testament in mind. For Jesus to fulfill the Old Testament means that he is bringing closure to the entire Old Testament story. God's story has reached its climax in the death and resurrection of the Son of God.

The disciples flee as Jesus is dragged away by a vengeful crowd. Now Jesus is left to face the religious leaders and then the Roman guard, despised, rejected, and abandoned. The Son of God is arrested like a criminal.

Begin by reading aloud:

　　　　Lesson 36: Jesus Doesn't Fight Back When Arrested

While he was still speaking, Judas, one of the Twelve, arrived. With him was a large crowd armed with swords and clubs, sent from the chief priests and the elders of the people. Now the betrayer had arranged a signal with them: "The one I kiss is the man; arrest him." Going at once to Jesus, Judas said, "Greetings, Rabbi!" and kissed him.

Jesus replied, "Friend, do what you came for."

Then the men stepped forward, seized Jesus, and arrested him. With that, one of Jesus' companions reached for his sword, drew it out, and struck the servant of the high priest, cutting off his ear.

"Put your sword back in its place," Jesus said to him, "for all who draw the sword will die by the sword. Do you think I cannot call on my Father, and he will at once put at my disposal more than twelve legions of angels? But how then would the Scriptures be fulfilled that say it must happen in this way?"

At that time Jesus said to the crowd, "Am I leading a rebellion, that you have come out with swords and clubs to capture me? Every day I sat in the temple courts teaching, and you did not arrest me. But this has all taken place that the writings of the prophets might be fulfilled." Then all the disciples deserted him and fled.

Just as Jesus finishes praying in Gethsemane, a large crowd carrying swords and clubs comes to arrest Jesus, as if he were a criminal. The crowd brings weapons because they probably think Jesus will have a lot of people there to fight against them. They still think that Jesus wants to be a king with soldiers and land, but they are wrong. Jesus will not fight them. His kingdom is not about war but telling people about God.

The crowd knows where to find Jesus because Judas, one of Jesus' disciples, betrayed him. When the crowd gets there, Judas goes over to Jesus and calls him "Rabbi." That means "my teacher," which is what the disciples always called Jesus. Then Judas kisses Jesus. Back then this was a normal way that people greeted each other, like a handshake today. But Judas is not just greeting Jesus. Earlier, Judas had told the crowd that the one he kisses is the one they should arrest. Kissing Jesus is a signal, not a greeting. That is how Judas betrays Jesus.

Jesus calls Judas "friend." Jesus really means this. Judas is one of his disciples, one of his twelve close friends. They went everywhere together for three years. They spent a lot of time talking, laughing, and praying together. They were friends and they loved each other. But now this friend is betraying Jesus to have Jesus arrested and killed. It is hard for us to imagine how hard it is for Jesus to have one of his friends betray him like this. Imagine hiding from some bullies who want to hurt you, and your very own brother tells the bullies where they can find you. If someone from your own family did this to you, your heart would be broken. That is how Jesus feels when Judas turns his back on him and betrays him to the leaders who want to kill him.

Before they take Jesus away, one of the three disciples causes some trouble. He takes his sword and cuts off the ear of the high priest's servant. This disciple wants to protect Jesus, but Jesus tells him to put the sword away. In Jesus' kingdom there is no fighting with swords. The disciple should have known that by now. Jesus' kingdom is about knowing God, loving him, and loving others. This is what Jesus has been teaching all along, even now when he is being arrested.

Jesus does not need to be protected anyway. If he wants to, he can snap his fingers and Jesus says God will send twelve legions of angels to surround him. A legion is 6,000 Roman soldiers, so twelve legions is 72,000. Jesus does not mean actually 72,000. He just means "as many as I want."

But Jesus does not want to call for help. He wants to do what God wants. Jesus will obey God and die on the cross. Jesus is the Son of God, but he lets the crowd arrest him like a criminal. He does not fight back.

     Lesson 36: Jesus Doesn't Fight Back When Arrested

The Rest of the Story

For the Parent: We did not want to end Year Two without giving an overview of how the story ends: with Jesus' trial, death, and resurrection. These three episodes will be revisited in detail in more advanced levels of this curriculum, but younger students should also get a clear sense of where the story of Jesus is ultimately going.

Matthew, Mark, and Luke all have their distinct ways of telling the story of the crucifixion and resurrection. These supplemental lessons, however, are all taken from John's Gospel, which includes some stories that are not included in the other Gospels (e.g., the "doubting Thomas" episode and the appearance to Mary). By focusing on John in the supplemental lessons, the children can get to know John's Jesus a bit better.

Lesson 1

John 19:1–16
A Politician Condemns an Innocent Man

What the Parent Should Know: In this story, Pilate, the Roman governor of Judea, is being pressured by the religious leaders to condemn to death Jesus, an innocent man. Pilate knows that he is caught between a political rock and a hard place. There is no just reason to put Jesus to death, but if he refuses to help the Jews uphold their laws, he will face possible rebellion, which would be more trouble than it's worth—not to mention attract the attention of Caesar, which might lead to questions of Pilate's fitness to rule. As politicians often do, Pilate is looking to keep the constituency happy for his own survival. He first tries to appease the demanding crowd by having Jesus beaten. But in the end, Pilate chooses political survival over justice by handing an innocent man over to be crucified.

As this scene opens, Pilate has just given in to the crowd's demand that he set free Barabbas, a political rebel (John 18:39–40, see Year One, Supplemental Lesson 1). Next Pilate hands Jesus over to be flogged and then mocked by wearing a crown of thorns and a purple "royal" robe. Flogging was a severe punishment, enough to cause death in some cases. Pilate hopes flogging will satisfy the crowd so that he can avoid ordering Jesus' execution. Pilate then presents Jesus in his ridiculous state to the crowd, but the religious leaders shout "Crucify! Crucify!" (v. 6). Exasperated, Pilate tells the leaders to crucify Jesus themselves, but this does not satisfy them. Jesus has committed blasphemy (v. 7), they claim, and according to Jewish law, he has to be put to death. Flogging is not enough, and only the Roman government has the authority to carry out the proper sentence.

The charge of blasphemy startles Pilate, for he can see that the Jewish law leaves him no alternative but to execute Jesus—unless he is able to interrogate Jesus and get him to credibly deny the charge. So, he begins his interrogation of Jesus. He asks Jesus "Where do you come from?" (v. 9)—no doubt hoping that Jesus will not claim some divine origin. Jesus had earlier engaged Pilate in a conversation (18:33–38), but now gives him no answer. This frustrates Pilate, who had the power to free Jesus if he so chose. But Jesus reminds Pilate that any power he has is at the true God's pleasure (v. 11).

This exchange convinces Pilate all the more that Jesus is innocent and needs to go free. So he goes back to the crowd and tries repeatedly to stem the tide against Jesus—without success. The crowd is now in a frenzy and beyond reason. They want Jesus dead because he is a blasphemer, and to get Pilate to do their bidding, they drop a political bomb on Pilate that seals Jesus' fate. Jesus claimed to be "King of the Jews." If Pilate lets Jesus go, Pilate himself will be committing treason against Caesar.

Pilate gives in to the fear of political reprisal and hands Jesus over to be crucified, even though he is clearly innocent. Despite the political tensions between Rome and the Jews, both forces converge to condemn to death an innocent man.

Then Pilate took Jesus and had him flogged. The soldiers twisted together a crown of thorns and put it on his head. They clothed him in a purple robe and went up to him again and again, saying, "Hail, king of the Jews!" And they struck him in the face.

Once more Pilate came out and said to the Jews, "Look, I am bringing him out to you to let you know that I find no basis for a charge against him." When Jesus came out wearing the crown of thorns and the purple robe, Pilate said to them, "Here is the man!"

As soon as the chief priests and their officials saw him, they shouted, "Crucify! Crucify!"

But Pilate answered, "You take him and crucify him. As for me, I find no basis for a charge against him."

The Jews insisted, "We have a law, and according to that law he must die, because he claimed to be the Son of God."

When Pilate heard this, he was even more afraid, and he went back inside the palace. "Where do you come from?" he asked Jesus, but Jesus gave him no answer. "Do you refuse to speak to me?" Pilate said. "Don't you realize I have power either to free you or to crucify you?"

Jesus answered, "You would have no power over me if it were not given to you from above. Therefore the one who handed me over to you is guilty of a greater sin."

From then on, Pilate tried to set Jesus free, but the Jews kept shouting, "If you let this man go, you are no friend of Caesar. Anyone who claims to be a king opposes Caesar."

When Pilate heard this, he brought Jesus out and sat down on the judge's seat at a place known as the Stone Pavement (which in Aramaic is Gabbatha). It was the day of Preparation of Passover Week, about the sixth hour.

"Here is your king," Pilate said to the Jews.

But they shouted, "Take him away! Take him away! Crucify him!"

"Shall I crucify your king?" Pilate asked.

"We have no king but Caesar," the chief priests answered.

Finally Pilate handed him over to them to be crucified.

In this story, Jesus is standing before Pilate, the Roman governor of the land of Judea who rules over all of the Jews. Pilate is deciding whether to have Jesus crucified or let him go free. The religious leaders want Jesus dead, but Pilate is trying to find a way to let Jesus go free. Pilate and the religious leaders argue back and forth, but at the end, Pilate hands Jesus over to be crucified. He does this because he is afraid of what the crowd will do to him if he lets Jesus go. Jesus is innocent, but Pilate condemns him to death anyway.

The religious leaders want Pilate to put Jesus to death because they say Jesus is guilty of a crime called blasphemy. Blasphemy means that a person claims to be God. In the Old Testament, the penalty for blasphemy is death. The religious leaders charge Jesus with blasphemy because Jesus has told the people all along that he could forgive sins, which is something only God can do. He also told people again and again he was equal to God. Jesus is telling the truth, but the Jewish leaders do not believe him, so they want him put to death. They need Pilate to do this, because only the Roman government can put people to death.

But Pilate does not care about Jewish laws like blasphemy. He only cares if Jesus has broken a Roman law. Jesus has done nothing wrong against the Roman government, and so Pilate says he will let Jesus go. But the religious leaders want Jesus crucified anyway. They are so loud and persistent about it that Pilate begins to see that he has a big problem on his hands. Jesus is innocent, but if he doesn't do what the crowd wants, they may try to rebel against him.

Pilate does not want a rebellion because, if they win, he could lose his power. He might even be killed himself. So, Pilate has Jesus flogged. He hopes that will be punishment enough for the crowd. Flogging is a severe and painful punishment. Prisoners are tied to a post and whipped so hard they almost die from it. After Jesus is flogged, Pilate makes fun of Jesus by dressing him in a purple robe that kings wear and a crown made up of thorns and presents Jesus to the crowd.

Jesus is nearly dead from the flogging and now looks ridiculous dressed up as a king. Pilate hopes that flogging and mocking will make the crowd forget about having Jesus put to death. But the crowd still wants Jesus dead no matter what. To get Pilate to put Jesus to death, they threaten Pilate. They say, "Jesus calls himself the king of the Jews. If you let Jesus go free, the Emperor Caesar will call you a rebel, too, because only Caesar is the true king."

This frightens Pilate more than anything. If Caesar is unhappy with him, Pilate may not only lose his throne—but his life. So, Pilate gives up trying to let Jesus go. He hands Jesus over to the guards to have Jesus crucified, even though he knows Jesus is innocent.

[Note to Parents: This lesson includes a brief description of crucifixion. We have made it as age-appropriate as possible, but we encourage you to preview the narration before presenting it to your child.]

What the Parent Should Know: This passage begins and ends by John saying that Jesus' death fulfills Scripture (vv. 28 and 36–37). The first is an allusion to one or two Psalms. At the end of the passage, there are two details of Jesus' death that John alone of the four Gospel writers mentions as specific fulfillments of the Old Testament: None of Jesus' bones would be broken and his body would be pierced. Through these allusions, John shows that Jesus' death is not an unfortunate tragedy but part of God's plan, echoed already in the Old Testament.

Knowing that his final moments are near, Jesus asks for something to drink. He is given some wine vinegar—the common man's wine—to drink. It is dipped in a sponge and lifted to him on a hyssop branch. John says that this act fulfills Scripture, though it is not clear which passage he has in mind. Likely we see here an echo of Psalm 22:15 ("My tongue sticks to the roof of my mouth") and 69:21 ("They put gall in my food and gave me vinegar for my thirst"). John and the other New Testament writers sometimes hear "echoes" of the Old Testament in something Jesus does or says. By alluding to the Old Testament here, John means that Jesus' suffering on the cross is not an accident but follows the Old Testament pattern spoken of in the Psalms.

After Jesus takes a drink, he says, "It is finished," and with that last utterance he dies. Jesus means more than just "My life is at an end." He means that, by his death, his mission in the world is complete. Jesus was sent by God to redeem the world (e.g., 3:16). Now that task is completed.

What remains now is for Jesus to be taken down from the cross and buried. John explains that Jesus dies on the "day of Preparation"(Friday), the day before the Sabbath (Saturday) when the Jews prepared ahead so that no work would need to be done on the Sabbath. In addition, this Sabbath was a "special Sabbath" (v. 31) because it coincided with the Passover. The Jews have every reason to make absolutely sure that the bodies do not remain on the cross once the sun goes down on Friday. To ensure quick death, they ask Pilate to break the legs of Jesus and the two men who had been crucified with him. Crucifixion is a slow process of asphyxiation where one's body weight prevents air from entering the lungs. The condemned rely on their ability to push themselves up with their legs in order to breathe. Breaking their legs ensures a more speedy (and even more painful) death.

The soldiers break the legs of the two men crucified with Jesus who are still alive. Since Jesus has already died, his legs are not broken. Instead, a soldier stabs Jesus in the side with a spear to make sure Jesus is dead. The blood and water that flow from the wound are normally explained as evidence that Jesus was literally pierced in the heart—the clear liquid is what filled the sac around the heart (pericardium, literally "around the heart"), whereas the blood is from the heart itself.

John, however, was not interested in such details from a medical standpoint. His focus was on how Jesus' death further echoed Israel's story in the Old Testament. John sees Jesus' intact legs as a fulfillment of the Passover law in Exodus 12:46 (see also Numbers 9:12 and Psalm 34:20), where none of the lamb's bones are to be broken. Jesus is the "lamb of God": his blood delivers the people from death, as did the Passover lamb (see Lesson 34).

John also sees the piercing of Jesus' side to be a fulfillment of Scripture, specifically Zechariah 12:10 (see also Isaiah 53:5). In Zechariah, the identity of the "one they have pierced" is a bit tricky to understand. In context, it probably refers to God himself being pierced by sorrow, although Jewish tradition came to understand the one pierced as the future messiah. John may be following both lines of thinking—God himself, in Jesus the Messiah, is pierced.

By linking Jesus' suffering and death to the Old Testament, John is saying that Jesus' death is not an afterthought or accident. Everything is proceeding according to plan. Jesus is the new Passover lamb, who suffers and is sacrificed on behalf of the people in fulfillment of Scripture.

Begin by reading aloud:

Later, knowing that all was now completed, and so that the Scripture would be fulfilled, Jesus said, "I am thirsty." A jar of wine vinegar was there, so they soaked a sponge in it, put the sponge on a stalk of the hyssop plant, and lifted it to Jesus' lips. When he had received the drink, Jesus said, "It is finished." With that, he bowed his head and gave up his spirit.

Now it was the day of Preparation, and the next day was to be a special Sabbath. Because the Jews did not want the bodies left on the crosses during the Sabbath, they asked Pilate to have the legs broken and the bodies taken down. The soldiers therefore came and broke the legs of the first man who had been crucified with Jesus, and then those of the other. But when they came to Jesus and found that he was already dead, they did not break his legs. Instead, one of the soldiers pierced Jesus' side with a spear, bringing a sudden flow of blood and water. The man who saw it has given testimony, and his testimony is true. He knows that he tells the truth, and he testifies so that you also may believe. These things happened so that the scripture would be fulfilled: "Not one of his bones will be broken," and, as another scripture says, "They will look on the one they have pierced."

This story tells us about Jesus' death. Jesus' followers are full of despair and sadness that Jesus is hanging on a cross, nearly dead. They do not understand how this could be happening to Jesus. They believe that Jesus is God's Son. How can God's Son come to such a horrible end, dying on a cross like a criminal?

John tells us that Jesus' death on the cross is not an accident but fulfills Scripture. That means that God knew all along that Jesus needed to die for our sins. John shows us that the Old Testament talks about Jesus' suffering.

So, John says that Scripture is fulfilled when Jesus says, "I am thirsty." In one of the psalms from the Old Testament, the writer of the psalm, David, is suffering because he is being attacked by his enemies. He is totally exhausted and in one verse he says, "My tongue sticks to the roof of my mouth." When John sees that Jesus is parched with thirst, he understands that the psalm is not just talking about David's suffering but Jesus', too.

After Jesus says "I am thirsty," someone (probably a soldier) takes a sponge, soaks it in wine vinegar, sticks the sponge on the end of a long branch, and holds it up to Jesus' mouth so he could drink. (Wine vinegar is a kind of wine that people drank back then instead of water, since water could be dirty, not filtered and purified as water is today.) After Jesus takes a drink, he says, "It is finished." Jesus means he is now finished with what God sent him to do. God loves the world, so he sent Jesus to die on the cross. Now that Jesus is about to die, he says, "I have done what God sent me to do."

Jesus has died, but the two criminals on either side of Jesus are still alive. This causes a problem for the Jews. It is Friday afternoon and the Sabbath begins at sundown, in just a few hours. The Old Testament law says that Jews may not work on the Sabbath—and that includes taking the bodies off of the crosses and preparing them for burial. So, they ask the Roman governor Pilate if they could break the legs of all three.

Why would they ask that? So that the three would die more quickly and they could be buried before the Sabbath started. The way someone dies when they are crucified is through asphyxiation—when you can't get enough air in your lungs. Hanging on a cross pulls the body's weight down, and the only way to keep breathing is to push up with the legs to get some air. If the criminals' legs are broken, they won't be able to push up and breathe. Breaking the legs will bring death more quickly, and that means that the Jews will be able to bury the bodies before the Sabbath begins.

When they get to Jesus, though, they see that he already looks like he is dead. So, instead of breaking his legs, a soldier stabs Jesus in the side with a spear to make sure he is actually dead.

The Gospel writer John sees two other ways that Jesus' death on the cross fulfills Scripture. The Old Testament says that the Passover Lamb is to be sacrificed but without any of its bones being broken. The Old Testament also says that, one day, the people in Jerusalem will look at God's servant and see him pierced with a spear. When John sees Jesus dying on the cross—with no broken bones and with a spear that pierced his side—John is reminded of what the Old Testament says and understands that Jesus' death is not an accident. Everything is happening according to God's plan as the Old Testament says.

<table>
<tr><td>Lesson
3</td><td>John 20:10–18
Mary Magdalene Spreads
the News that Jesus is Alive</td></tr>
</table>

What the Parent Should Know: John is the only Gospel that records this encounter between Jesus and Mary Magdalene. Mary is the one who sees Jesus first after his resurrection, although she does not recognize him at first. After she hears Jesus' voice, Mary realizes that the man in front of her is the risen Jesus. Mary alone brings the news of the resurrection to the disciples.

In the previous passage, Peter and John (called "the other disciple" in 20:2) have seen that the tomb was empty, but they still do not understand what has happened (20:9). They return to their home, but Mary remains at the entrance of the tomb, crying. (The Greek word means "wailing" in grief and mourning.) Mary sees two angels seated in the tomb where the head and feet of Jesus had been. They ask her why she is crying. Mary does not recognize that they are angels. She simply answers that Jesus' body was taken away, and that she does not know where it is (v. 13). Like the disciples, Mary has no idea that Jesus has been raised from the dead; she assumes Jesus' body was stolen.

When Mary turns around, she sees Jesus but thinks he is a gardener—again, the thought of Jesus being alive is not even on her radar screen. The only explanation she can think of for the empty tomb was that the body has been removed, either by this "gardener" or someone else.

Mary does not recognize Jesus by sight, but when Jesus speaks Mary's name she finally knows who is standing before her. Recognizing Jesus by his voice appears earlier in John's Gospel, in 10:3: "The sheep listen to his voice. He calls his sheep by name and leads them out." Upon recognizing Jesus, Mary addresses him with the familiar Aramaic title "Rabboni." Aramaic was the main language of Jews at the time, and Rabboni—as John himself explains—means "teacher" (or perhaps "my teacher"). This title only occurs elsewhere in the New Testament in Mark 10:51. It means the same thing as "Rabbi," which is a common word used in the Gospels to refer to Jesus.

Mary then either hugs him or is about to, but Jesus tells her no. His reason is a bit cryptic: "for I have not yet returned to the Father." Scholars have pondered long and hard what is happening here. Some think that Mary is trying to "hold on" to Jesus—to keep him from going away a second time. A better explanation is that Jesus is in a rush to have Mary bring the news to the disciples because his time on earth is limited (according to Acts 1:3, the ascension took place forty days after the resurrection). In other words, to paraphrase v. 17, Jesus means, "Stop wasting time holding on to me. I am returning to the Father soon, so you'd better get a move on and start spreading the news."

Mary alone remains at the tomb and sees the risen Jesus. Now her task is to hurry off and tell the disciples that Jesus will soon be returning to where he came from. There is no time to waste spreading the news: Jesus is alive.

Begin by reading aloud:

Today's story begins on Sunday. Jesus was crucified on Friday, and his body has been in the tomb for the last two days. The Jewish Sabbath began Friday night and lasted until Saturday night, and Jews were not allowed to do any work on the Sabbath. So, the disciples had to wait until Sunday morning to come to Jesus' tomb. And when they arrive Sunday morning, they see that the tomb is empty. Jesus is gone, and they cannot believe their eyes. Even though Jesus has told them all of this was going to happen, they don't understand. So the disciples go back to their homes. But Mary stays behind. She will be the one to tell all the others that Jesus is no longer dead, but alive.

Then the disciples went back to their homes, but Mary stood outside the tomb crying. As she wept, she bent over to look into the tomb and saw two angels in white, seated where Jesus' body had been, one at the head and the other at the foot.

They asked her, "Woman, why are you crying?"

"They have taken my Lord away," she said, "and I don't know where they have put him." At this, she turned around and saw Jesus standing there, but she did not realize that it was Jesus.

"Woman," he said, "why are you crying? Who is it you are looking for?"

Thinking he was the gardener, she said, "Sir, if you have carried him away, tell me where you have put him, and I will get him."

Jesus said to her, "Mary."

She turned toward him and cried out in Aramaic, "Rabboni!" (which means Teacher).

Jesus said, "Do not hold on to me, for I have not yet returned to the Father. Go instead to my brothers and tell them, 'I am returning to my Father and your Father, to my God and your God.' "

Mary Magdalene went to the disciples with the news: "I have seen the Lord!" And she told them that he had said these things to her.

Mary is alone at the tomb of Jesus. Jesus' body is gone and she does not know what has happened to Jesus. So she stands outside the empty tomb and cries—not softly but loudly. She is wailing because she is so distressed that Jesus was crucified and now on top of that his body is missing. Who would do such a horrible thing and take Jesus' body?

Then Mary sees two angels sitting in the empty tomb—one angel is sitting where Jesus' head was and the other where Jesus' feet were. Mary does not know they are angels. They ask her why she is crying, and she says, "Someone took Jesus' body and I don't know where it is."

Mary turns around and sees Jesus standing there, but she doesn't recognize him, either. She doesn't understand what Jesus had told all the disciples about rising from the dead. Mary just doesn't expect to see Jesus standing there. She thinks he is a gardener.

But then Jesus calls Mary by her name. At last, she recognizes him. She calls him "Rabboni." That is an Aramaic word that means "teacher" (Aramaic is the language that the Jews spoke.) "Teacher" is what Mary and the disciples always called Jesus.

If you were sad like Mary and then saw Jesus, who you thought was dead, what would you do? Mary goes over to hug Jesus. Has one of your parents ever gone away on a long trip, and then they finally come home? When you see them you run up and hold on to them because you are so happy to see them. Mary thought Jesus was gone forever, but now he is back.

But Jesus tells her not to hold on to him. He tells Mary this because he wants her to run right away to spread the news. Jesus is alive, and that is great news! There is no time to waste.

Index